JOY in JESUS

How to pin down, catch and keep
what most Christians miss out on

DAVID MARSHALL

AUTUMN
HOUSE

All quotations come from the New International Version
(Hodder and Stoughton, copyrights 1973, 1978 and 1984,
International Bible Society) unless indication is given to
the contrary.

Copyright © 1998 by David Marshall

First published in 1998

British Library Cataloguing in Publication Data.
A catalogue record for this book is available
from the British Library.

ISBN 1-873796-74-9

Published by
AUTUMN HOUSE
Alma Park, Grantham, Lincs, England,
NG31 9SL

ACKNOWLEDGEMENTS

I should like to acknowledge, with gratitude, the help of Miss Nan Tucker, Professor John Walton, Dr Hugh Dunton, Mrs Isobel Webster and Pastor R. H. Surridge in critiquing this book in MS form. Thanks are also due to Mrs Gloria Barradine and Mrs Anita Marshall for setting the MS, and to Mr Barrymore Bell for proof-reading it.

DEDICATION

To Anita

'I enjoyed reading JOY IN JESUS. Not only did I enjoy it, but I found it a blessing. Many of the things I read, spoke to my heart.'

RONALD H. SURRIDGE
professor emeritus
Newbold College

ABBREVIATIONS

KJV	King James Version (1611)
RSV	Revised Standard Version (Oxford, 1952)
NRSV	New Revised Standard Version (Oxford, 1989)
NIV	New International Version (Hodder and Stoughton, 1979)
NEB	New English Bible (Oxford and Cambridge, 1961)
REB	Revised English Bible (Oxford and Cambridge, 1989)
LB	Living Bible (Tyndale House, 1971)
NLT	New Living Translation (Tyndale House, 1996)
JBP	J. B. Phillips, The New Testament in Modern English (Collins, 1972)
GNB	Good News Bible, Today's English Version (Collins/Fontana, 1976)
NASB	New American Standard Bible (A. J. Holman Company, 1973)

CONTENTS

WANTED
A JOY EXPLOSION!

My theme was 'Joy Unspeakable', and I was well into it. The church fathers who designed the pulpit had not had short preachers in mind; so, as I warmed to my theme, I was on tip-toe to give me maximum exposure to the congregation. The congregation knew what that meant and ninety-and-nine faces beamed at me. *I had them!*

But who was the fellow at the back taking notes? (Always an unnerving practice!)

As I moved on into Philippians, Paul's Epistle of Joy, I enthused, 'What the Christian Church needs above anything right now is a JOY TRANSFUSION!'

Suddenly, my ninety-and-nine became a hundred! In a trice, he dropped his lap top, leaped to his feet, shot a clenched-fisted right hand into the air and, from a joy-full face, yelled: 'YES-S-S! YES-S-S!'

This chap I had to meet, and did.

He came from Glasgow, and had an interesting tale to tell. He was a committed Christian himself and, over a number of years, had made it his business to worship with 1,400 congregations, across forty-two denominations, over Britain, Ireland and North America.

To my surprise, I found him to be an introvert, somewhat em-barrassed at his own outburst. 'You're right!' he said. 'I've been trying to nail it down, the missing ingredient, the greatest need — AND IT'S JOY!' He had made charts, graphs; listed faults, suggestions, points of comparison. But had been bothered by a bogy: What was the missing link? It was, he had decided, a lack of joy.

Yet Joy was so central to the teaching of Jesus. Joy (*makarios*) was the most oft-repeated word in the Sermon on the Mount. The words joy and rejoicing are part of the punch-line of the majority of parables.

Joy was a constant in the life and writing of Paul. From the death cell of a Roman prison, he exhorted the Christians in Philippi to be a people of joy!

Within hours of His arrest, Jesus made a promise to Christians of every age, including ours: ' "These things I have spoken to you, that my joy may be in you, and that your joy may be full. . . . No one will take your joy from you. . . . Ask, and you will receive, that your joy may be full." ' John 15:11; 16:22, 24, RSV.

Is this a gift on offer, but unasked for, not experienced?

Warren W. Wiersbe writes: 'Those who have trusted Christ have the privilege of experiencing "fulness of joy" (Psalm 16:11, RSV). Yet few Christians take advantage of this privilege. They live under a cloud of disappointment when they could be walking in the sunshine of joy.' *Philippians: Be Joyful* (Scripture Press).

YES-S-S! YES-S-S!

And let's make reading about joy a route to experiencing joy!

Joy is the heart of the Christian's experience. Joy is the key to the verve of worship — and church growth!

Charles R. Swindoll writes: 'Most (yes, most) Christians you and I know have very little dynamic or joy in their lives. Just ask them.' *Flying Closer to the Flame* (Nelson Word).

WANTED: A JOY EXPLOSION!

THIS BOOK COULD MAKE ALL THE DIFFERENCE

JOY IN JESUS is a book that speaks to the basic human desire for permanent happiness from the word 'go'. Its crisp, refreshing style urges the reader to move without pause from one chapter to the other.

For the reader living in the fast lane its content can be absorbed by bedtime while, for the more leisurely person, its fascination can be imbibed at a slower pace.

Each page deals with this scarce commodity *joy unspeakable* as deriving from a divine-human relationship and an awareness of one's own spiritual needs.

The exposition of the beatitudes as an agenda for happiness defines not so much what joy is but who are the joyous ones. Among those who are the truly happy ones are: the humble in spirit, the meek, the pure in heart, and those conscious of their need for righteousness.

The argument is compelling as the apostle Paul is brought into the picture as one who depicted the qualities enumerated by Jesus on the Mount. In the face of Roman cruelty and religious persecution Paul is portrayed as maintaining an inexplicable joy in the Lord. The secret of his peace is attributed not to self-assurance but assurance in Jesus Christ.

The graphic description of the violinist losing all the strings of his instrument save one is reminiscent of untold human experiences in which we choose either to play or to abandon hope. As demonstrated in this case, the harmony of life can be played on one string but it depends on the player. In the Master's hand the life left with a single choice through brokenness can become a symphony of joy. These important insights on how to buck the trend and become a joyful Christian are like nuggets of gold to be cherished, not wasted.

The enemies of joy are exposed and the source of genuine joy established. Joy is not only desirable but possible in the human experience.

Reading this book could make a difference between the misery of negative introspection and a life of genuine, lasting joy in Jesus.

CECIL R. PERRY

THE GIFT OF JOY

In a rash moment when I was 15, I promised God I'd go and work for Him. Then, almost immediately, I had second thoughts. In those distant days, 'working for God' meant entering the ministry; and the ministry, to one adolescent mind at least, had a serious image-problem.

In the Nonconformist denomination in which I was raised, all the clergy – correction, all the clergy *I* knew – wore black suits, black ties, black shoes, black socks, black hats and, in one notorious instance, a very long black coat! But that wasn't the worst of it. They also wore long white faces and looked as if they might well hold down a night job at the local mortuary!

That, to me, reflected an all-serious attitude towards life which I felt I could not live with. As a consequence, I took my well-exercised sense of humour to university rather than to Bible college, and became a teacher of teenagers.

To be involved in the planting of a new congregation is an exciting experience, even to a teacher of teenagers. There came a time when a spot of retraining seemed to be called for. Nevertheless, even when it was completed, enough of the old image-problem of the clergy was still in my thinking, to cause me to give considerable prayer and thought before accepting ordination. What clinched it for me, I still believe, was an example of God's direct intervention in my life. In the course of one evening, it seemed to me that He drew my attention to two Bible verses, one from each Testament. The first was part of a picture of God's ransomed people entering Zion. It concluded with the words, '"Everlasting joy will crown their heads. Gladness and joy will overtake them."' Isaiah 51:11. The second was from the mouth of Jesus Himself; 'Your joy no man taketh from you.' John 16:22, KJV.

The words of Jesus were, so far as I was concerned, conclusive. It was then that I realized that God's indestructible joy could not only be taken into the ministry, but was indispensable to a minister.

It was about the same time that I realized that the black-suited brigade of my youth had not, themselves, been entirely joy-free. They had, however, assumed a persona which they doubtless thought appropriate to clergymen, and joy had not figured prominently in their output. One of my favourite Christian writers says, 'Nothing in all religious history has done Christianity more harm than its connection with black clothes and long faces.'

I recalled those events while waiting to be interviewed on a London radio station. Charles Swindoll, waiting to record his programme, told me how he first became involved in radio ministry in the US. In his case black suits were not a problem. The thing that made him fight an offer of a radio programme was the persona of the typical US radio/TV evangelist. 'It was that super-pious, religious-fanatic bit that I couldn't handle,' he said. 'They appeared to be hyper intense about everything . . . .'

Fortunately for Christian broadcasting, somebody made it clear to Swindoll that he could conduct his programme in his inimitable joy-filled way. Within weeks of being on the air Swindoll was inundated with bumper bundles of mail. The following letter he quoted to me as typical: 'I appreciate your programme. The teaching has helped me a lot . . . but I have one major request: Don't stop laughing! You can stop teaching, and you can make whatever other changes you want, but *don't* stop laughing.' And then the part of the letter that griped his gizzard: *'Yours is the only laughter that comes into our home.'* What has created a joy-free generation? When did stress, tension and pressure replace laughter? When was it that joy, once the glue of family life, departed to leave hearts that seldom sing, lips that rarely smile, eyes that no longer dance, and faces that say 'No'?

There seems to be little distinction between the Christian and the non-Christian home on this one. What a tragedy!

Yes, the times are tough. No question. We must come to grips with issues that are serious and real. Yes; some days bad news is the *only* news. Yes; there are joy-stealers, faith-crushers and grace-busters by the score – and they are *inside* the Church.

So where does joy come in?

Joy is the Sanity Clause. Even more importantly, joy is the key to a fulfilling spiritual experience.

Joy is a gift – as far as God is concerned.

Joy is a choice – as far as you are concerned.

And joy is a gift God wants all of us to choose. . . .

I was flying out to a Middle Eastern country. My itinerary involved meetings with some highfalutin people and interviews with a couple of people whose names were, at that time, almost household words. That was the positive part. Not quite so positive, as we touched down in the heat-felted darkness of an almost-deserted airport, was the fact that the flight, scheduled to arrive at 10pm, was actually touching down at 2.30am, that forty miles of desert separated me from my billet and that, as everyone knew, that country had a vast underclass of people with little respect for the rule of law.

Against the odds, I made it – luggage intact – to my billet within an hour! Decanted by the driver of a 1953 Morris outside my modest (Christian) hostel, I then became conscious of another problem. On an earlier visit to that place, in order to get some great night-time shots of a Middle Eastern capital, I had climbed out of my window on to a flat roof. In doing so, I had walked through a beam and set off a terrorist alarm. The whole building throbbed with noise! At length, I was apprehended by a burly Scotsman who, within a couple of years, would be Moderator of the Church of Scotland! But that night there was nothing 'moderate' about him. He was a crime-buster

and, in his mind, I was a criminal. Only the timely intervention of someone who knew me had saved me from the
cells!

If that could happen before nine o'clock in the evening, what
would happen if I succeeded in rousing everyone at 3.30am? I
began to envisage what would occur if I started to assault that
large door with my fists, in an effort to raise the warden at that
ungodly hour.

I nerved myself.

But the door opened as if by faith alone. Looking down, I
saw a short lady in a serious, heavy-duty dressing-gown – but
with a smile on her face that almost illuminated the dark night.
In an instant, my insecurities and loneliness fled. In a glorious
Scottish accent she said, 'Dr Marshall, I'd almost given you up
for lost! I'm so pleased to see you.' Within minutes, I had a hot
drink in my hand and within half an hour was deep in the
restorative sleep that would prepare me for the challenges of the
coming day.

Once my journalistic assignments were over, by prior
arrangement I joined a party led by University of Michigan
archaeologist, Dr William Shea.

The next weeks were spent chasing Dr Shea and his party
around the archaeological sites of the Middle East. His
schedule was frantic, and I left and returned at all kinds of
hours (all of them unsocial). But the little lady with the mood-
shattering smile was always there, as was the smile. Breakfast
at 5.30am; she had the porridge prepared for me (well, nobody's
perfect!). At 1am, the smile still intact, she was there to open
the door and welcome me home.

Rarely have I encountered such an even, thoroughly happy
person.

For the last week of my visit I was joined by my wife. The
days were more leisured and we had an opportunity to get to
know Carole very well. She looked 28 but was, as it turned

out, 48! (At the time 48 seemed an amazingly advanced age to me!)

The night came to depart. And, yes, it was a *night* departure. Britain-bound planes from that country seemed able to take off only under cover of darkness.

Before we left our hostel to catch that middle-of-the-night flight, I had to ask her for her secret. How could she keep it up? That even, thoroughly happy disposition; that mood-blasting, tiredness-dispelling, security-instilling, happiness-making smile?

She told me her secret. The smile was undimmed, but there was also a certain coy modesty. 'You see,' she said, 'the Lord Jesus has given me the Gift of Joy . . . .'

Carole's wide-open eyes sparkled.

On the way home in the plane I couldn't forget it:

The Gift of Joy.

Charles Haddon Spurgeon, a preacher and teacher of preachers, said this to his ministerial students: 'An individual who has no joy about him had better be an undertaker and bury the dead for he will never succeed in influencing the living . . . .'

'Your joy,' said Jesus, 'no man taketh from you.'

That's the Sanity Clause.

It's also the key to the most fulfilling kind of life that can be lived on this planet.

Remember:

Joy is a gift, as far as God is concerned.

As far as *you* are concerned, joy is a choice.

And it's a choice that has to be exercised a hundred times a day.

WHERE THERE'S ONLY ONE STRING

Niccolo Paganini was a great violinist. He was also a natural Italian showman. Fiddling through a complicated piece in front of 5,000 people, he suddenly heard a *ping!* – and knew that a string of his violin had snapped.

With the skill of a master – but not without sweating a bit! – Paganini improvised beautifully. Then *ping!* – another string had snapped, quickly followed by a third. The strings hung down limply. What could the great violinist do with the one remaining string?

Paganini completed the composition on one string!

The Italian audience went wild. Someone yelled, 'Encore!'

Paganini turned to the conductor and winked. To the audience he shouted, 'Paganini – and one string!' holding up his Stradivarius. Then he placed the instrument under his chin and played the final piece on *one* string, while conductor and audience shook their heads in amazement.

Victor Frankl was one of the Jews who survived the Holocaust. At the time of his arrest, no one would have predicted his survival. His enemies had removed his possessions, destroyed his home and sent his family to their deaths. The Gestapo shaved his head, stripped the clothing from his body and marched him into a courtroom to be interrogated and falsely accused. Totally destitute, Frankl was helpless in the hands of sadistic men. He had nothing. No; that's not quite true. He had one thing. Frankl had the power to choose his own attitude. To give up or to go on. Bitterness or forgiveness. Hatred or hope. Determination to endure or the paralysis of self-pity. It came down to: 'Frankl . . . and one string!'

It is difficult adequately to express the importance of the choice of attitude upon life. It has been said that life is 10 per cent what happens to us and 90 per cent how we respond to it. Attitude is the single string. My attitude is more important than my past, my education, my bank account, my successes or failures, my fame or pain, what other people think of me or say about me, my circumstances or my position. It is my 'single string' that fuels my fire or assaults my hope. When my attitudes are right, there's no barrier too high, no valley too deep, no challenge too great. . . .

Nevertheless, we expend a disproportionate amount of time and nervous energy over the strings that snap, dangle and pop: • the weather; • people's actions and reactions, especially the criticisms; • delays in traffic, at airports, in waiting rooms; • the price of everything from groceries to airline tickets; • on-the-job irritations, disappointments, workloads.

The greatest waste of energy has to be fighting the inevitables! As a result, circumstances totally beyond our control can come to determine our moods, rob us of humour, affect our decisions, influence our judgement, sour our social relationships, be a major factor in bringing about our success or failure – in our professions or businesses, as parents or marriage partners – and become an influential factor in determining our mental and physical health, and the quality and quantity of life.

Stress, anger, discontent, irritation, frustration, impatience – all create a situation in which our chemical-producing pituitary and adrenal glands may have some difficulty keeping up with demand. Our reserves of adaptation energy are not unlimited. So how you are determines *who* you are! Make too many withdrawals and the results could be irreversible chemical scars and premature ageing.

Further, the body reacts to vast amounts of chemicals released into the circulatory system. The body's internal surfaces are affected. Tissue function is disrupted. The negative impact will be on the body's weakest point. If it is the lining of the stomach – and it often is – stomach aches and diarrhoea or even ulcers may result. If the moving surfaces of the joints become inflamed, arthritis may be the consequence. With some people it may be headaches or high blood pressure.

Once it was thought that relaxation and/or exercise were adequate correctives. Recent research indicates that the choice depends on the extent of the damage done – as well as on the diet, blood cholesterol, alcohol consumption and a score of other lifestyle factors.

And it's all down to getting strung up on the strings that snap, instead of making melody with the one that remains. You are, after all is said and done, performing on a Stradivarius!

Whatever happens, you have a choice – of attitude!

Philippi was a city in Macedonia founded by Philip, the father of Alexander the Great. There Antony and Octavian defeated Brutus and Cassius, the assassins of Julius Caesar. There, in August AD 50, an ageing Jew from Tarsus, Paul, founded a multi-cultural, multi-ethnic Christian Church. Paul wrote a letter to that church fourteen years later while awaiting execution.

The substance of Paul's famous last words?

Attitudes.

And if anyone was qualified to write about attitudes it was Paul.

It was said of Paul and his companions that they had turned the world upside down. And that was no idle over-statement.

But Paul had been in prison for the six years before he wrote to the Philippians.

His arrest had been occasioned by a popular rising against him in Jerusalem. That, in turn, had been orchestrated by his enemies who had spread false gossip about him. Paul had every reason to feel a powerful sense of injustice.

The initial stages of the legal process had been mishandled

and Paul became the victim of conspiracy. His own people were plotting to murder him. He had every reason to feel vengeful and frustrated.

He was imprisoned by the Romans in Caesarea. His hearing was before Governor Antonius Felix. Paul was left in no doubt by that most venal of time-servers that a handsome bribe would sort everything out. Paul didn't hand out bribes. His case was adjourned – *for two years!* He had every reason for cynicism and anger.

When Governor Porcius Festus heard his case, the Prosecution team employed by Paul's enemies manipulated the system so effectively that he felt he had no alternative but to appeal to Caesar (his right as a Roman citizen). By then he could have been seriously stressed out; cheated, the victim of a trumped-up charge, based on an almost forgotten lie – a loser.

The journey to Rome took eight months. As a prisoner under guard he found that his advice was ignored. As a direct consequence, the flimsy vessel was caught up in a storm – and wrecked. By then doubt and anger might have soured his relationship even with God.

A period of house arrest in Rome was probably followed by a trial before a court that didn't understand the charge! The occasion of his second trial was probably the Fire of Rome. Nero wanted someone to blame and the Christians were so unpopular they were the custom-made, no-questions-asked victims.

In the first chapter of his letter to the Philippians, Paul mentioned four times that he was 'in chains'. He felt, he said, as if his life were already being poured out like a sacrificial drink offering (2:17). Ahead: execution.

Self-pity time, surely? Time to give in to the one-hundred-and-one dark moods? Any letter written then would surely be vicious with bitterness, a plea to the influential Latins in the Philippian church to help arrange his escape, release, to make him an exception to the anti-Christian pogrom because of his social status?

No, to all of the above.

No, to all and every negative attitude.

Paul wrote to the Philippians the most upbeat letter in the New Testament. They were to have the attitude of Jesus – and be a people of joy.

On the one string left to him, Paul played a symphony without a single discordant note. And it was a symphony of joy!

THE JOY AGENDA OF JESUS

The nine 'beatitudes' (Matthew 5:3-12) with which Jesus begins the Sermon on the Mount, outline His recipe for joy. In them we discover the agenda of the Christian who, having encountered the good news, can proceed to live life to the full: to maximize his joy. 'You have heard the Gospel,' Jesus is saying. 'And the Gospel brings joy in the here-and-now world as well as life everlasting. Here's how!'

'And he opened his mouth, and taught them.' (5:2, KJV.) In centuries past, He had opened the mouths of prophets – Isaiah, Jeremiah, Ezekiel, Daniel. Now Jesus, the Word made flesh, God among us, 'opened his mouth and taught them, saying, *"Blessed"*'.

Makarios joy. Christian writers have spent gallons of ink explaining *agape*, the love of Jesus and the beyond-comprehension *shalom* peace of Jesus. They have spent little explaining *makarios,* the joy of Jesus.

It is even possible that Bible translators have done less than justice to the joy of Jesus.

Perhaps 'blessed' was a fair enough approximation in 1611 when the Authorised Version was published, but is it possible that the coinage of blessing is a bit debased these days? When we're surprised, it's 'Bless me!' When it's mealtimes, it's 'Bless the food!' When it's prayer time, it's 'Bless the pastors and the missionaries' and – maybe – 'the royal family', and – certainly– '*our* family'. When someone sneezes, it's 'Bless you!'

'Blessed' is not what it was.

Therefore, modern translations have opted for 'Happy'. But is it an improvement?

'The greatest happiness of the greatest number is the foundation of morals and of legislation,' wrote Utilitarian philosopher Jeremy Bentham. Yes? 'Different men seek after happiness in different ways and by different means,' said Aristotle. Where does that leave us? 'Happiness is like a sunbeam, which the least shadow intercepts,' says the inevitable Ancient Chinese Proverb. And there's something in that. The Ancient Greek Euripides (writing in 408BC) agreed: 'Happiness is brief. It will not stay.' All Americans have the inalienable right to 'Life, Liberty and the Pursuit of Happiness', but have you seen CNN and watched their movies? 'Modern man's happiness consists in the thrill of looking at the shop windows, and in buying all that he can afford to buy, either for cash or on instalments.' That was Erich Fromm in *The Art of Loving*.

Is it possible that 'H-A-P-P-Y' is not just debased and overused, but simply the wrong word for God's *makarios* joy?

Makarios – translated either 'blessed' or 'happy' – means 'the joy of God; a deep sense of contentment and wellbeing'. A sense, in fact, that you can have even in the midst of hostile or uncomfortable circumstances – because it is not dependent on circumstances.

So 'happy', frankly, just won't do!

'Happy' comes from the Anglo-Saxon word *hap*, meaning 'chance'. 'Mayhap', they say in Yorkshire: 'By chance.' 'A happenstance,' they say in the US: 'A chance occurrence.' (*Webster's Dictionary.*)

Happiness is, you might say, a chancy business. Life may give it and life may take it away. It is dependent on a whole raft of variables: your health, your sex life, the success of your plans and ambitions, the mood of your spouse, the viability of your car engine . . . .

Now stand back for William Barclay's definition of *makarios* joy, the joy of Jesus:

Makarios joy is 'that joy which seeks us through our pain, that joy which sorrow and loss, and pain and grief, are powerless to touch, that joy which shines through tears, and which nothing in life or death can take away.' William Barclay, *The Daily Study Bible: Matthew 1* (Revised edition 1975), page 89.

Christians are often accused of offering the joy of the hereafter as a compensation for the stern, puritan life they feel called upon to live now. No. *Makarios* joy is a present-tense joy, and a joy you can enjoy when the present is tense. It is a joy that the hazards and sorrows of life are powerless to touch. '"No one,"' said Jesus, '"will take your joy from you."'(John 16:22, RSV.) So the stern, puritan life is, in itself, a denial of the joy of Jesus. Walking in the presence of Jesus provides the Christian with a serene and untouchable joy – in the NOW. A deep, bedrock joy, that nobody can shift, because it is divine.

God's congratulations. The beatitudes, then, are God's congratulations.

They are not just statements; they are exclamations. English versions of the beatitudes supply the verb *are*. It isn't there in the Greek. Jesus, of course, was speaking in neither English nor Greek, but in Aramaic (a form of Hebrew). That being the case, it is very likely indeed that Jesus was using a form of exclamation repeatedly employed in the Psalms.

With a clear understanding of the meaning of *makarios* joy, and taking on board the fact that the beatitudes were intended as exclamations, we can present the beatitudes like this:

• Oh the joy of those who have realized their total inability to help themselves, who have placed their complete trust in God: theirs is the kingdom of heaven.

• Oh the joy of those who repent of and renounce their sins: the Comforter will come to them.

• Oh the joy of those who meekly accept Jesus as Saviour and Lord: they will inherit the earth.

• Oh the joy of those who, with new life, have new appetites – who hunger and thirst after righteousness: they will be filled.

• Oh the joy of those who are merciful: they will be shown mercy.

• Oh the joy of those with undivided hearts: they will see God.

• Oh the joy of those who share God's peace formula: they will be called God's children.

• Oh the joy of those who are persecuted because they stand up for what is right: the kingdom of heaven is theirs.

• Oh the joy of those who are insulted, misunderstood and maligned for Christ's sake: they stand in line with history's best and greatest – and that is where they belong!

Do you begin to see how Paul survived imprisonment, disaster, injustice, pain and torture – and remained joyful? His joy was the *makarios* joy of Jesus, the cast-iron joy that external circumstances cannot erode or dissolve. How, exactly, had he come by it?

WHERE JOY BEGINS

The prospect of imminent death is said to concentrate the mind wonderfully. As Paul waited for Nero's sentence to be carried out, what did his wonderfully-concentrated mind produce?

Attack from the back. One's whole life is also supposed to flash before one's eyes as death comes close.

So with Nero and a sharp sword in his immediate future, it is not surprising that the past should have figured in Paul's thinking. Though preoccupied with the immediate problem being faced by the Philippian Christians, Paul chose the details of his own early life and background to make his point.

From the start of Paul's ministry, he had been followed around by the activists of a pseudo-Christian cult opposed to the Good News he was preaching. Those cult followers believed that Paul's preaching – salvation through Christ alone – was inadequate. Paul's gospel, they believed, was at best the 'first stage' in a salvation process for the Gentile converts. To achieve 'maturity', they said, those Gentile converts had to add to Christ's righteousness an unblemished track record of their own. Nothing less than perfect law-keeping was required, and it had to begin with the symbolic rite of circumcision.[1]

That 'Christ-Plus-Performance' cult had been causing confusion and taking the joy out of the experience of Paul's converts since his very first missionary journey. Then, in prison awaiting execution, Paul had heard news about the destructive work of the cultists among the believers in Philippi.

Paul was broad-shouldered enough to say, 'What does it matter if they are preaching the gospel from wrong motives? Or sniping at me? Or getting too big for their boots? At least Christ is being preached! All the other stuff I'll leave God to sort out.' (See Philippians 1:15-18.) 'If we take any other view,' Paul is saying, 'then we allow them to steal our joy . . . .'

But there was one point at which Paul dug in his heels and wouldn't budge. People who messed with the messenger could be ignored – no big deal. People who messed with the message, on the other hand, could expect exposure and reprimand in the strongest possible terms.

Salvation = Christ + nothing, Paul insisted. Those who added Performance to Christ robbed the Christian of his joy, and undervalued Christ and Calvary, grace and love. To the Galatians he had denounced those 'infiltrators' as 'sham Christians' and 'false brothers' (Galatians 2:4, NIV, NEB) who preached 'a different gospel – which is really no gospel at all' (1:6, 7). Twice, for emphasis, Paul said they should be 'eternally condemned' (1:8, 9).

Paul had written to the Galatians at the beginning of his ministry. He was writing to the Philippians right at the very end. Had his anger at those who perverted the Gospel mellowed with time? Far from it. In the midst of the Epistle of Joy, Paul issued a fierce warning against the circumcision-legalists: 'Watch out for those dogs, those men who do evil . . . .' (3:2.) Strong language! Remember, 'dogs' in Paul's day were not house-trained pets. They were dirty, disease-carrying scavengers who ran in packs through the streets and alleys of the city. Paul warned: 'Beware! These people will savage you and you will lose your joy!'

Then, drawing on his own story, Paul explained why – facing imminent execution – he was so stirred up about those perverters of God's good news.

Flashback. Salvation was possible through Christ's sacrifice alone. Nothing needed to be added to His righteousness. Then, turning feisty, Paul said that if salvation by performance had been possible then *he* would have made it! His pedigree was impeccable! A Jew par excellence! Circumcised on the eighth day; bearing in his person a mark that indicated that he was one of the Chosen and entitled to be a part of the Covenant. Of the tribe of Benjamin; and Benjamin had had a unique place in the history of Israel – it was from Benjamin that the first king of Israel had been chosen and Paul (Greek equivalent of Saul) had been named after him. Benjamin was the only one of the patriarchs actually born in the Land of Promise. When Israel went into battle, it was the tribe of Benjamin that held the post of honour (3:4-6).

Paul's pedigree was not only as an Israelite; he was of the aristocracy of Israel. 'A Hebrew of the Hebrews' was how Paul expressed it. In other words, not one of the Jews of the Diaspora who, in a foreign land, had forgotten his own tongue. Paul was a thoroughbred; he both remembered and used the language of his fathers. Better, even, than that, 'in regard to the law' Paul was 'a Pharisee'. Before his Damascus-road experience, Paul had not only been a devout Jew, but one of the exclusive brethren, 'the separated ones', who forswore all normal activity in order to dedicate life to the keeping of the law, taking meticulous care to ensure blamelessness on all points.

In terms of the 'legalistic righteousness' of the circumcision cult, Paul scored 101! He had the Oscars, the Pulitzer Prizes, the Grammys, the Emmys – even the Nobel Prize for Performance-Righteousness! (See Philippians 3:2-6.)

As Paul had ridden to Damascus to capture the Christians, the streak of pride down his back was so broad you could have rented space on it!

All that was before his encounter with the risen Christ. That encounter had blown all his pride, all his human righteousness, and all his drive for earthly applause clean away. In place of his 101 score, he dropped down to zilch. 'Whatever was to my profit I now consider loss for the sake of Christ. What is more, I consider everything a loss compared to the surpassing greatness of knowing Christ Jesus my Lord, for whose sake I have lost all things. I consider them rubbish, that I may gain Christ and be found in him, not having a righteousness of my own that comes from the law, but that which is through faith in Christ – the righteousness that comes from God and is by faith.' Philippians 3:7-9.

The impeccable pedigree? Rubbish! Circumcision, the sign of the Chosen? Rubbish! His family, tribe, education, national origin? Irrelevant! His performance righteousness? 'Dung!' (3:8, KJV). At best, dirty washing. (See Isaiah 64:6.)

Was Paul wallowing in low self-worth?

Far from it!

Paul was defining salvation's first base.

He was where it all starts. The point where God can begin to work on a man.

All of which explains why Jesus began the beatitudes with the words . . .

'Blessed are the poor in spirit.'

Here begins our lasting joy!

Remember *makarios* joy?

Some time ago we conducted a door-to-door survey in Hemel Hempstead. We started with, 'Which TV programmes do you watch?' 'What sort of music do you like?' The point of the exercise was to learn how much people knew about Jesus. But about halfway down the survey was the question, 'What is your main aim in life?' On the answer to this one there was an amazing consensus: 'To be happy.' When we pressed for a def-inition of happiness it involved the 'deep *makarios* joy' that Jesus offers here to the poor in spirit.

Further down in the survey, it was shocking to learn how little people knew, or cared, about Jesus.

But the answer to that question halfway down the survey was what boosted my spirits. People might have spent sixty hours a week glued to the goggle-box, blasting their brains out with hard Rock, clambering up the ladder of materialism, filling

thought-free days with soap operatics, trivial talk and grab-
bing and grasping for things with which to fill life's super-
market trolley – but what they *really* wanted was something
that only Jesus could provide. They wanted *real* joy. They
wanted *makarios* joy.

And right at the top of the joy agenda of Jesus are the words:
'Oh the joy of the poor in spirit.'

A moment before he met the risen Christ, Paul would have
considered himself 'rich in spirit' and, asked for evidence,
would have listed the points of his pedigree, his Oscars, his
Grammys and his Emmys. Or should we say, his Very
Reverends, Most Reverends and Right Reverends? Faced with
the only perfect One, he knew that his spirit was empty, that
he had nothing to offer God – and, through the years of his
ministry, what roused his ire more than anything else was when
he heard from people who believed they could impress God
with their performance, earn salvation with their efforts. Paul
knew that the kingdom of heaven was reserved for the poor
in spirit.

The law leads to Christ. In ancient Greece a *pedagogue* was
employed to lead and protect (presumably unwilling) children
on their way to school. Paul said that the function of the law was
to be the *pedagogue* 'to lead us to Christ that we might be justified by faith'. (Galatians 3:24.) The law cannot save, never
forgives, and has no propelling energy.

Paul summarized the message with which he and his Spirit-
powered followers turned the world upside down, in these
words from the book of Romans: 'But now God has shown us
a different way to heaven – not by "being good enough" and
trying to keep his laws, but by a new way (though not new, really, for the Scriptures told us about it long ago). Now God says
He will accept and acquit us – declare us "not guilty" – if we
trust Jesus Christ to take away our sins. And we can all be saved

in this same way by coming to Christ, no matter who we are or what we have been like.' Romans 3:19-22, LB.

No one can ever be made right in God's sight by doing what the law commands. In this very Sermon on the Mount, Jesus was to add the dimensions of thought and motive to the law.[2] The law not only required that I *do* good, but that I *be* good; not only demanded that I be squeaky-clean on the outside – but pure in thought and motive on the inside. A man who harboured hatred was guilty of murder. A man who looked lustfully on a woman was guilty of adultery. (Matthew 5:18-28.) Only when we recognize the full extent of the law's demands are we broken. For the more we know of God's laws, the clearer it becomes that we aren't obeying them; His laws serve only to make us see that we are poor in spirit – sinners – with nothing of ourselves with which we can merit salvation:

'Blessed are the poor in spirit' –

Gone is self-sufficiency.

'Blessed are they that mourn' –

Gone is self-satisfaction.

'Blessed are the meek' –

Gone is self-will.

'Blessed are they who hunger and thirst after righteousness' –

Gone is self-righteousness.

These four beatitudes describe what happens when we are converted. And conversion has to begin when we recognize our poverty of spirit.

That Survey in Hemel Hempstead demonstrated emphatically that the *real* desire of the great majority of people was for the lasting joy that Christ provides. But you will have noticed that the word employed by those we surveyed was, actually, 'happiness'. How do you think most people pursue happiness? Sex, sport, food, fashion, entertainment: things that, in the main, satisfy the body or, possibly, occupy the mind, or at least a part of it. But man is made up of body, mind and spirit. Real joy will come about only when we give as much attention to the spirit as we do to the other two. And the first step in that direction is when we acknowledge its poverty.

The final question in the Survey was, 'Are you really happy?' From an impressive survey of 1,200, no one gave an unqualified 'Yes'. Why? Their pursuit of happiness lay in pleasing the body while ignoring the spirit. And that, by the by, is why some of the most wealthy people in the world are among the most miserable!

The first step to real joy? To be honest enough to acknowledge to myself, and to God, that I don't have what it takes to be the person I know I ought to be. Paul acknowledged that the very things he wanted to do were the very things he did not do. And the things he did not want to do were the things he did. Poverty of spirit involves identifying with Paul's dilemma – *and* with his conclusion: 'I know that nothing good lives in me.' Paul concludes his self-disclosure with these words, 'What a miserable person I am! Who will free me from this life that is dominated by sin?' Then he answers his own question: 'Thank God! The answer is in Jesus Christ our Lord. . . . ' Romans 7:14-25; (See especially verses 18, 24 and 25, NIV, NLT.)

Outside in. In an interview given not long before his death the actor Sir Lawrence Olivier admitted that when 'becoming a part' he worked from 'the outside in'. He started with the externals – the make-up, the false nose, the mannerisms, the accent – and from there sought to reach the core of the part. The truth is, of course, that although he acted the part, and did so brilliantly, he never *became* the part. No actor ever did. Even in his best performance he was only an actor. Someone pretending to be someone else.

To someone who acknowledges his poverty of spirit, God is in a position to work a revolution – from the inside out. This change, though gradual, is so total that Jesus referred to it as a 'new birth' (John 3:3-17). The inside-out approach begins with man's acknowledgement of his spiritual poverty.

As God gradually transforms us, can we then become more and more proud of our spiritual maturity? In AD48, at the outset of his ministry, Paul introduced himself to the Galatians as: 'an apostle – sent not from men nor by man, but by Jesus Christ and God the Father'. (Galatians 1:1.) After seven years, during which God had worked to renew his mind, Paul wrote to the Corinthians: 'For I am the least of the apostles and do not even deserve to be called an apostle.' (1 Corinthians 15:9.) After a further eight years of the refining influence of the Holy Spirit, Paul assessed himself 'less than the least of all God's people'. (Ephesians 3:8.) Finally, in one of his prison letters, Paul wrote, 'Christ Jesus came into the world to save sinners – of whom I am the worst.' (1 Timothy 1:15.)

The first step on the road to real joy is to recognize the poverty of spirit; that Jesus is not an optional extra but is 100 per cent indispensable in every area of life.

Paul first acknowledged his poverty of spirit as he looked into the face of the risen Jesus. That he continued to acknowledge his poverty of spirit is neither accidental nor coincidental. First, it indicates that he was getting to know his Saviour better and better as the years went by. Second, it indicates that, as the Holy Spirit had greater access to his mind and heart, the ideals he had for himself became more and more exalted.

The beatitudes represent a progression in the Christian's experience. It is significant that the first and last beatitudes conclude with the words, 'For theirs is the kingdom of heaven.'

Jesus can make what is poor in spirit rich. To the person who honestly acknowledges his poverty of spirit, all the riches of the kingdom of heaven are available. Right from day one.

[1]Howard Marshall, *The Epistle to the Philippians* (Epworth, 1992), page 75. [2]John Stott, *The Message of the Sermon on the Mount* (IVP, 1988), pages 36-37.

EN ROUTE TO JOY

Dag Hammarskjöld was Secretary General to the United Nations when I was a boy. He was more widely respected in the international community than any other Secretary General has been. The poet W. H. Auden called him 'a great, good and lovable man', and Auden did not dish out praise willy-nilly. By contrast, Hammarskjöld, in his autobiography, *Markings,* wrote of 'that dark counter centre of evil in my nature'.

John Newton was the captain of a slave ship, plying the notorious 'Middle Passage' between West Africa and the West Indies in which, so appalling were conditions, two-thirds of those being transported died. Newton accepted Christ as his Saviour, repented of the heinous wickedness in which he had been involved and, after training, accepted ordination to the Anglican ministry. Some years into his ministry, and having written a number of hymns including Amazing Grace, Newton wrote this in his private diary: 'I am not what I ought to be! Ah! how imperfect and deficient! I am not what I wish to be! I am not what I hope to be!'

The eighteenth-century New England revivalist Jonathan Edwards wrote: 'When I look into my heart and take a look at its wickedness, it seems like an abyss infinitely deeper than hell.'

Augustus Toplady, a well-known cleric (now chiefly remembered for his hymns) wrote this in *his* diary at the end of 1767, 'During the past year I desire to confess that my unfaithfulness has been exceeding great. My sins still greater . . . .'

The twentieth-century Christian communicator, C. S. Lewis, found within himself 'a zoo of lusts, a bedlam of ambitions, a nursery of fears, a harem of fondled hatreds'.[1]

Jesus – indispensable. Round about here is where you begin to shake your head and say to yourself, 'Er . . . I thought this book was about joy . . . .'

It is.

Honestly!

The road to lasting, bedrock joy begins at the point when you acknowledge your poverty of spirit. At the point where, like Paul, you admit that the only good thing about you is Jesus Christ (Romans 7:18, 24).

Joy begins when you realize Jesus is 100 per cent indispensable to your life.

Once you have accepted your poverty of spirit, you have to square up to it, and *mourn it.*

Jesus' second 'beatitude'? 'Blessed are those who mourn, for they will be comforted.' Matthew 5:4.

Oh, the *joy* of the *mournful?*

Yes! Yes!

Stay with me!

Mourning for sin. The Old Testament often used mourning as a picture of repentance. Typical is Ezra who, in confession, threw himself down before the house of God and wept. 'A large crowd of Israelites – men, women and children – gathered round him. They too wept bitterly.' Ezra 10:1. They had acknowledged their spiritual bankruptcy, their inability to help themselves, that they were undeserving of God's grace – *and they mourned!*

In the New Testament, Paul, having given the Corinthians an unabridged account of exactly what they were doing wrong, told them they had no right to be proud – *they should be in mourning!* (1 Corinthians 5:2, RSV.)

Mourning for sin and emptiness is the second step on the road to joy!

The sorrow of the second beatitude is sin-sorrow: repentance. Acknowledging spiritual poverty is one thing. Actually grieving over it is quite another. You are not only saying, 'I'm sorry for what I've done,' but 'I'm desperately sorry for what I am.' Though sorry for what you've done, you may do it again in a few hours or days. Being sorry for what you *are* is saying, 'Lord, without You my sinful nature will destroy me. Self-sufficiency and independence are not an option. I need to live in dependence on You. On my own I'll sink beneath the fathomless depths of evil. I have no strength or resources, God – I need Yours!'

The defining moment. Paul talked about a reservoir of evil within man (Romans 3:21-24). So did pagan philosopher Plato: 'There's a blind, many-headed monster that is all that is evil within you.' Dr Samuel Johnson wrote: 'Every man knows that about himself that he would not willingly tell his best friend.'

Luther felt weighed down by Paul's description of 'the righteousness of God' and the sinfulness of man. There were tortured years in which he felt condemned by it, and terrified.

Before Augustus Toplady collided with his spiritual poverty and began to mourn, he was noted as the most arrogant cleric of his generation. John Wesley and George Whitefield were leading a revival that affected the whole of the British Isles and overspilled into the Americas. And it made Toplady seriously angry! The Gospel of Wesley and Whitefield, like Paul's, was the Gospel of grace. Their most outspoken critic was Toplady. His letters and sermons were pure vituperation. His pride prevented him from accepting that a man could be saved independently of his performance.

But Toplady's theology changed, suddenly, completely. He lived in an age before cars and bicycles when a country parson travelled either on horseback or on foot. One night, walking through Burrington Coombe, the rock rising vertically on either side of the path, Toplady was caught in a tremendous thunderstorm. He found shelter in the cleft of a rock. It took some time for the storm to abate. And it was in that period of time that

Toplady had his theology turned round and, after that, his whole life. He commemorated his turn-round in verse:

> 'Not the labour of my hands
> Can fulfil thy laws demands:
> Could my zeal no respite know,
> Could my tears for ever flow,
> All for sin could not atone;
> Thou must save, and thou alone.

> 'Rock of Ages, cleft for me,
> Let me hide myself in thee;
> Let the water and the blood,
> From thy wounded side which flowed,
> Be of sin the double cure,
> Save me from its guilt and power.'

Two of the lines in another verse of Toplady's hymn – 'Nothing in my hand I bring, simply to thy cross I cling' – were frequently quoted in the sermons of the great nineteenth-century preacher Charles Haddon Spurgeon. One member of his congregation became so tired of hearing these lines that one evening he passed a note to the preacher which read, 'We are sufficiently informed about the vacuity of your hand . . . .' At the earliest opportunity Spurgeon responded, '"Sufficiently informed" you may be, but is it part of your experience?'

The biggest barrier on the joy road is spiritual pride: the belief that we can achieve/deserve salvation. When we reach a point where we acknowledge that this is simply not possible, we begin to mourn.

The blessing. Jesus says that those who mourn will be 'comforted'. Elsewhere, He calls the Holy Spirit the 'Comforter'. When we mourn our poverty of spirit, the Holy Spirit is free to start working in our lives, and to begin to live in our lives the life of Jesus. When we mourn our poverty of spirit, the Holy

Spirit begins to replace our weakness with the strength of Christ. He changes our sin for the righteousness of Christ and our defeat for the victory of Christ. And that is *very* comforting! When the Gospel realization comes, it is also very joyful!

Writing to Ephesus, Paul reminded the Christians of the foundation of their joy: 'I keep asking that the God of our Lord Jesus Christ, the glorious Father, may give you the Spirit of wisdom and revelation, so that you may know him better. I pray also that the eyes of your heart may be enlightened in order that you may know the hope to which he has called you, the riches of his glorious inheritance, . . . and his incomparably great power for us who believe.' Paul prayed that the defining moment might come for all the Christians in Ephesus, that they might mourn their sin and the Spirit might direct their lives (Ephesians 1:17-19). Then Paul expressed the joy of the Gospel as briefly, succinctly, as you will find it expressed anywhere: 'For it is by grace you have been saved, through faith – and this is not from yourselves, it is the gift of God – not by works, so that no one can boast.' Ephesians 2:8, 9.

After tortured years – intimidated by 'the righteousness of God' – Martin Luther came to know the joy of the justified. He realized that 'the righteousness of God' (Romans 3:21-24) was 'the righteousness *from* God': a gift to those who mourned their sin and held out the empty hand of faith. Instead of viewing God as a vengeful deity, he came to see Him as the Father in the Prodigal Son story. When Luther grasped that the righteousness from God – the only *genuine* kind of righteousness – was *'apart from law'* (performance, track record) and was God's gift, he caused the biggest explosion of joy in Christian history since the first century. We call it the Reformation.

When John Newton, acknowledged that he was not what he ought to be, what he wished to be, or what he hoped to be, he reached *his* defining moment: 'Though I am not what I ought to be, nor what I wish to be, nor what I hope to be, I can truly say I am not what I once was, a slave to sin and Satan, and can heartily join with the apostle, and acknowledge, '"By the grace of God, I am what I am!"' It was *that* that gave him something to sing about in Amazing Grace!

By the time Toplady came to review the year 1767 in his diary, he had reached *his* defining moment. His unfaithfulness had been 'exceeding great', his sins 'still greater'. But this is how he continued: 'God's mercy is greater than both. My short-comings, my misdoings, my unbelief and my lack of love would sink me to the lowest hell, were it not for Jesus my Righteousness and my Redeemer.'

But before his reaching this joyful conclusion, there had been mourning.

The first sign that the defining moment has occurred, that poverty of spirit has been mourned, is joy – then meekness!

The meek. 'Blessed are the meek,' said Jesus, 'for they will inherit the earth.' Matthew 5:5.

Once you have accepted Christ as Sovereign and Saviour, once the Spirit dwells within, then you begin to live the Christian life. Soon, and very soon, you come to know the joy of meekness.

Martyn Lloyd-Jones wrote: 'Meekness is essentially a true view of oneself, expressing itself in attitude and conduct with respect to others. . . . The man who is truly meek is the one who is truly amazed that God and man can think of him as well as they do and treat him as well as they do.'[2]

John Stott wrote, 'It seems important to note that in the Beatitudes "the meek" come between those who mourn over sin and those who hunger and thirst over righteousness.' We can, said Stott, learn something from this sequence; as we mourn for our sin we develop a humble and gentle attitude to others which is determined (Stott's words) 'by a true estimate of ourselves'.[3] The Hollywood/TV soap image of Christian meekness is a kind of weak effeminacy. We are invited to believe that, for the Christian, life is not fun but fanaticism. You won't meet many real live Christians like that.

Those who have given over their lives to God as Sovereign and Saviour are invited by Jesus to be joyful, fun people, ever at the start of a great adventure. Submission to God, in meekness, means accepting His agenda. And, His plans for your life are never dull but fresh, vibrant and exciting. Some people find them *too* exciting!

And God's plans begin now, not in eternity. Right here; the meek, remember, will inherit *the earth*. Social climbers may boast and materialists may build, but possession is beyond their grasp. In God's scheme of things, those who appear to 'have nothing' can, in fact, 'possess everything' (2 Corinthians 6:10).

You don't feel as if you've inherited the earth? And that that inheritance has given you aim, purpose and joy?

Perhaps it is because you do not have meekness. This, in turn, may be because you are not mourning, have not allowed Christ to clean and rebuild you. And this, in turn, may be because your pride is standing in the way of an acknowledgement of spiritual poverty. This acknowledgement, you may recall, is where the joy road begins. . . .

[1]Cited in William Griffin, *C. S. Lewis: The Authentic Voice* (Lion, 1988), page 65. [2]Martyn Lloyd-Jones, *Studies in the Sermon on the Mount* (IVP, 1959), volume 1, pages 68, 69. [3]John Stott, *The Message of the Sermon on the Mount* (IVP, 1988), pages 43, 44.

BE ATTITUDES AND *DO* ATTITUDES

I'm sorry for you. Yes, really! You see, the best comedians were all in my class at school. The chances are that you weren't. So you missed out on them!

Two are worthy of special mention: Terry Teesdale and Fatty Walton. (No, and *he* wasn't politically correct, either! He just had a healthy appetite about him!)

Ever since I left school I've been expecting them to make it big in the entertainment business. They never have. Maybe their clean, hilarious humour went out of fashion. One less than hilarious impact they had was that, having sat on either side of me in Maths and Physics, they lost me a couple of grades in those subjects. It was well worth it!

Everything was funny in those days. Life was meant to be enjoyed. At what point, exactly, did everything become so deadly serious?

Then there was home, another barrel of laughter. Dad worked for British Railways, in those days notoriously bad payers. To feed a family which, in post-War Britain was unfashionably large, in his spare time he maintained two gardens and an allotment. To clothe us he swept chimneys, had a sideline in mail order, and sold children's books door to door.

Looking back, we were definitely 'poor'. But, not for the most fleeting picosecond did that cross the mind of any of us, even though, on a daily basis – because there was never just the family at home – Ma had to perform a miracle which must have seemed like feeding the 5,000.

In the house we had an organ, a piano, an awful violin, hi-fi, a piano accordion, plus an oft-used instrument Dad called his 'squash box'. So we had plenty of 'music'! There was lots of laughing, too, and much joy. This had been true even when Hitler had made an airborne attempt to alter the local topography and town plan, and we had had to spend our nights under a large dining table. 'You're not scared of Mr Hitler, are you, Ma?' 'No fear!' *And* we had believed her!

Of course, Jesus was part of the family, too. It said so over the fireplace. He was 'The Unseen Guest At Every Meal', but He didn't eat much. We always asked Him to bless and multiply the food, and no one will ever convince me that He didn't oblige on a regular basis.

What's happened to families like ours? There were quite a few around in those days.

'Get real!' somebody says. And what's 'real' when it's at home? Why sacrifice joy on the altar of 'real'?

When *did* life become so very serious? The FT Index and the DOW become so tediously triumphant? Monetarist policy, and the health of the dollar and the pound sterling take top priority? When *did* the GNP, the Rate of Inflation, an accelerating crime rate, the decline of the NHS, the antics of terrorists, and the private lives of royals, politicians and soap stars become such an all-consuming preoccupation?

Look at the commuter crowd – or, for that matter, the consumer crowd in the shopping mall – tomorrow. Why *is* life for so many a marathon of frowns? If the charities caught on to The Sponsored Frown – as they have the sponsored bike ride/walk/ toddle/silence/swim – they could still outstrip the National Lottery!

Did the Big Switch happen when the nibs enshrined the precept 'Blessed are the pushy, assertive, and those that trample on the toes/fingers/heads of others – for first place in the rat race is theirs'?

The Jesus Agenda, you may recall, favours those who realize their utter helplessness, those who are sorry enough to quit, and the meek. He promised them the earth and all the joy they could handle. 'And your joy', He said, 'no one can take from you.'

That joy would be multiplied, says Jesus, by those with Blessed Attitudes. He pointed out three in particular. Having blessed the meek – without meekness there is no such thing as love, for the beginning of love is a sense of unworthiness – He said:

- **'Oh the joy of the one who longs for total righteousness as the starving long for food and those perishing of thirst long for water, for he/she will be truly satisfied.'**[1]

While you were still a sinner, in grace God offered you salvation. His offer was made possible by the death of Christ on the Cross. That was how the atonement came about: at-one-ment (2 Corinthians 5:21; Hebrews 9:22; 1 Corinthians 1:30). Through the strange transaction at the heart of the Gospel, you left at the Cross both your sins *and* your feeble attempts at DIY righteousness. In exchange, you received the righteousness of the Sinless One. That's salvation in a nutshell.

The first evidence that you are saved? Changed appetites. This is what Jesus is saying here.

The evidence that you are a Christian is not so much what you believe, but how you behave. 'This is how we know who the children of God are and who the children of the devil are: Anyone who does not do what is right is not a child of God; neither is anyone who does not love his brother. . . . We know that we have passed from death to life, because we love our brothers. Anyone who does not love remains in death.' 1 John 3:10, 14. All clear so far?

The average family in the Palestine of Jesus' day was a lot nearer the borderline of real hunger and actual starvation – authentic poverty – than my family ever was. It knew what it was to be hungry. And, having been caught out in many a sand-storm, it knew what it was to be parched with an imperious thirst. So when Jesus said that real joy belonged to those who 'hunger and thirst after righteousness', it knew He was not talk-ing about being 'peckish' or 'about ready for elevenses'.

Conversion is evidenced in changed appetites. And they, in turn, are evidenced in changed lives.

An appetite for righteousness means that the tax dodger stops dodging; the backbiter stops biting; the social climber lives by a new set of priorities. The picture is clear. Yes?

So suddenly everything's hunky-dory? Yes?

No! The devil doesn't give up that easily! Those who claim to live without sin are lying to themselves and to everyone else (1 John 1:10). We shall fall short of God's ideal – even of our own ideals – and echo Paul's 'Oh wretched man that I am' speech scores of times a day. That's when the 1 John 1:9 promise assumes priority: 'If we confess our sins, he is faithful and just and will forgive us our sins and purify us from all unrighteousness.' In short, when we fall down on the Joy Road, He picks us up, dusts us off – and we start all over again.

But the wonderful thing for those who mourn their sins, and continue to mourn every tumble they take along the way, is that God's Holy Spirit is the power and force for good within them. And 'the fruit of the Spirit is love, joy, peace, patience, kindness, goodness, faithfulness, gentleness and self-control'. Galatians 5:22, 23.

Those who acknowledge their powerlessness, mourn their sins and are meek have the 'in Christ' experience. Those who are 'in Christ' have Christ in them. They live life in the Spirit. They need fear no condemnation (Romans 8:1-4).

The Way of Joy has two great enemies: *Legalism,* at one extreme, and *Carelessness,* at the other. The Legalist never acknowledges that he cannot reach heaven by dint of hard slog; not getting past the 'poor in spirit' stage, he never embarks upon the Joy Road. The careless Christian is one who learns to mourn and be meek, up to a point; but loses sight of the supernatural element – the importance of the 'in Christ' experience and of the Spirit within. As a consequence, short of hungering and thirsting for righteousness, he experiences a return of the old appetites, loses his taste for (in the truest sense) the 'good life' and, in the process, misses out on the joy of salvation.

- **'Oh the joy of the one who learns what it's like to walk in another man's moccasins – see life from the other man's perspective – for that one will find that others do the same for him, and he will come to know what God has done in Jesus Christ.'[2]**

Mercy, the second Blessed Attitude, is compassion for the needy. As 'grace' deals with our sin and guilt, 'mercy' deals with what we see of pain, misery and distress, the results of sin.[3]

Jesus said that those who show mercy will be shown mercy; that those who forgive will be forgiven (Matthew 5:7; 6:14). 'This is not because we can merit mercy by mercy or forgiveness by forgiveness, but because we cannot receive the mercy and forgiveness of God unless we repent, and we cannot claim to have repented of *our* sins if we are unmerciful towards the sins of *others*.'[4] Nothing moves us to forgive like the awesome knowledge of the extent to which we ourselves have been forgiven. There is no clearer indicator that we have been forgiven than our own readiness to forgive.

No Christian who is the genuine article will either be unmerciful or unforgiving.

Jesus was very firm on this one. His parable on the subject – in Matthew 18:21-35 – is quite a shocker.

Peter brought up the theme of forgiveness. The Jewish rabbis taught that you should forgive your brother three times. So Peter doubled it, added one for the pot, and beamed at Jesus, expecting to be congratulated: 'How many times should I forgive my brother, Lord? Would seven times be enough?' Jesus responded, doubtless smiling broadly, with the words: 'More like seventy times seven!' And then He told His parable to illustrate *why* there is no limit to forgiveness.

A servant owed millions of pounds to his king. The figure Jesus gave was bigger than the annual tax bill for Judaea, Samaria and Galilee added together. A humungous sum. The exaggerated size of the debt is the whole point; a man's debt to God is so great he can never pay it back.

The servant with the humungous debt fell to his knees and begged for mercy. Actually, what he asked for was a special kind of mercy. What he said amounts to this: 'Master, give me a bit more time and I'll pay you everything.'

The servant's idea of forgiveness was one thing, the master's another. He didn't give him extra time to pay – *he cancelled the debt.*

But here's the crunch. *The servant could not accept the gift he was being offered.* He behaved as if he had just been given an extension of the time to pay. He found somebody who owed him a few measly pounds, grabbed him by the throat, said, 'Pay up!' and, when he couldn't, threw him into the debtors' prison.

This is where the shocking part of the parable comes in. Jesus said that the master threw the first servant into prison and gave him over to the torturers. Worse to come; He then makes it clear that that is how God will deal with those who do not forgive their fellow men and women from their hearts.

Who are these 'torturers' to whom the unforgiving are handed over?

Back in the days when trousers were flared and ties were kippered, the Welsh Rugby Union side was in the world-beating class. This was largely because of the 'Fearsome Foursome': Mervyn Davies, J. P. R. Williams, Gareth Edwards and Barry John. After a famous grand-slam victory, one newspaper reported, 'Half a ton of human flesh simply buried the opposition . . . .'

Jesus was saying that the unforgiven and the unforgiving are turned over to another Fearsome Foursome: *Guilt, Resentment, Striving, Anxiety.* These four produce emotional problems, warped personalities and breakdowns of relationships. The two major causes of emotional/psychological/spiritual problems among Christians today – *the two great joy killers* – are:

1. The failure to understand, receive and live God's unconditional grace and forgiveness.

2. The failure to give out that unconditional love, forgiveness and grace in relationships with other people.

Too many Christians, having placed their burden at the foot of the Cross, take it up again. Too many Christians, having renounced DIY righteousness, then start practising it as a lifestyle. Too many Christians miss out on mercy and, missing out on mercy, they inescapably miss out on joy.

- **'Oh the joy of the one whose motives are entirely unmixed, for he/she will some day see God Himself!'**[5]

This is where Jesus talks about 'the pure in heart'. Three different words in the New Testament are translated 'pure'. The word used for 'pure' here is not a word that means perfect. It's a word that means 'unmixed'. It was a word used in the context of harvest. When the grain had gone through the threshing process and had been separated from the chaff, all that was left was grain; 'pure grain' – not grade A grain, necessarily, but grain unmixed with chaff.

That great sinner King David prayed, 'Give me an undivided heart . . . .' Psalm 86:11.

Paul, in his Epistle of Joy to the Philippians, prefaced his pursuit of the things of God with these words, 'This one thing I do . . . .' Christians are apt to say, 'These 101 things I dabble with: one of them is my Christianity, one of them my career, one of them my recreation . . . .' When Paul said, 'This one thing I do,' that didn't mean to say that he didn't have any other recreation or interest. Paul was a well-read, well-rounded man. What he was saying was this: 'Whatever I do, whether it's connected with my career, my family or my social life, or any other thing, I live to please Jesus Christ.'

Those who want to be blessed with the joy of Jesus cannot compartmentalize their lives into, for example, secular and spiritual. Jesus has to be Lord of all. If He is not Lord of all, He will not be Lord at all. And service to the Lord of all is, in many cases, work for Him in the person of the least of these His brothers and sisters with whom He so closely identifies. In one powerful New Testament picture, all in primary colours, the last judgement is represented as turning on the issue of how we have related to the Lord in the person of the most vulnerable of His brothers and sisters (see Matthew 25:31-46).

Many prominent figures, with time and funds to spare, serve the vulnerable – with half an eye on the New Year or Birthday Honours lists. And equivalent recognition is not alien to the motives of a good many ordinary Christians. In the sermon of which the Beatitudes are the beginning, Jesus could not have been more swingeing about this sort of 'service' (Matthew 6:1-3).

'Blessed are the pure in heart' invites us to undertake a spot of self-examination. Self-analysis of this sort can be a mite uncomfortable. As I found a year or two ago. I had to admit to myself that a great deal of what I did 'for the Lord' was from a complex mixture of motives. Since the Spirit pointed that out to me, I have had this prayer written in the front of my diary: 'Unscramble my motives, Lord, that I may purer, simpler be.'

Changed appetites. A life of service. Unmixed motives.

These are the three Blessed Attitudes that mark the Christian and make his joy.

[1]See William Barclay, *The Daily Study Bible: Gospel of Matthew,* volume 1 (St Andrew Press), page 97. [2]See Ibid, page 100. [3]John Stott, *The Message of the Sermon on the Mount* (IVP, 1988), page 47. [4]Ibid. [5]See William Barclay, op cit, page 103.

THE WAR IS OVER

Much of the city looks as if it were built yesterday by some giant who freaked out on Lego. High-rise flats and offices dominate the skyline.

But by the river, in the dockland area, time has stood still. The refuse of bygone ages shifts in the wind through the arteries of a once-thriving commercial community. Now the Georgian façades, crumbled and melancholy, hide the haunts of old winos, loons, jades and beggars of every description.

Time was when, in search of higher learning among the Lego, I picked my way delicately through the winos and the beggars, the Georgian façades and the bombsites, in search of a ferry across the river. I spent many luggage-encumbered hours by the gangway to the floating pontoon, peering into the fog of the estuary for the appearance of the familiar paddle steamer. Those hours gave me more opportunity than I welcomed at the time to imbibe the salt spray, the ozone and the atmosphere.

The man in the shelter. By the gangway was a sea-shaken, brick-built shelter facing the estuary. Around it slunk the city's human jetsam who looked as if they might disconnect my freckles for the price of a whisky. In it sat one solitary man. *Always the same man.* Rain, shine, snow or blow he was always there. On wild winter nights, when the North Sea threatened to sweep his shelter out of the estuary, he was there. On bitterly cold mornings when Jack Frost had been out riming the railings, he was there. On balmy summer evenings, moon-dry, silent and airless, he was there.

He was in late middle age, tall, and dressed in a shabby trench coat. His eyes were always fixed on some distant point of the horizon.

What was he looking for?

Why was he there?

Regardless of storm or tempest, this voyager gave that man and his shelter a wide berth at all times.

There was deep unhappiness engraved on that face. And something more – undefinable, ghastly.

One day in late summer, when tides were unusually low, I sat out of doors munching on an unappetizing sandwich. Puritans populated my mind; they were the stuff of my current research project. And thunder rolled and reverberated over hills of cloud . . . .

'They're coppin' it at Dunkirk.'

In my preoccupation, I had been only dimly aware that a presence had settled down beside me. I was now only too aware that it had a voice. *It was he.*

'You got back all right, then? So did I,' he was saying. 'There was bombs and shells and bullets. Don't know how we made it, but we did. . . . Got back home . . . whole street bombed out . . . our house, a direct hit . . . wife and kids gone, mother buried alive. . . . George and Frank, me brothers, still in the thick of the shindy . . . expectin' 'em back. . . . This might be them now.'

As the ferry disgorged its human cargo – trippers, shoppers, commuters – he searched the face of every man in the crowd for the features of George and Frank. . . .

How many times had he gone through this ritual? How many times had that look of abject disappointment set in? What kept alive the hope that two long-lost brothers would return? Where did he spend his nights? Who fed him?

In the earnestness of youth, and before I realized that he sensed and felt and thought and experienced, but did not hear, I tried to tell him. *The war was over.* It had been over for more than twenty years. Dunkirk had receded into history.

All that filled *his* ears was the sound of gunfire, shells

thundering, bullets whining, voices calling, frantically. . . .

The war was over. But not in *his* head.

'Oh the joy of the peacemakers . . . .' The Joy Road begins when I face up to my poverty of spirit; that in myself I am incapable of being the kind of person I want to be. The joy bursts out when, having recognized that poverty, I *mourn* it; I turn away from doing it my way, to doing it God's way – and the Holy Spirit enters my life. The first evidence that the joy has really set in is when I say, in meekness, 'Lord, You are Sovereign; make my life Your mission.' A fulfilled, joyful life begins here; I inherit the earth. I have new appetites; I hunger and thirst after righteousness – not new experiences. Merciful to others, I am shown mercy; forgiving, I am forgiven. Single-minded in pursuit of Christ's mission in my life and in the world – 'This one thing I do' – I become a part of the solution, instead of being a part of the problem; the salt that savours, adds taste and tang; God's light in a darkened world; a diffuser of joy in a world depressed.

Then, as a remade man – 'a new creation' – I am commissioned by God to be His peacemaker in whatever context I find myself.

At the Cross I have learned God's peace formula. Now, on the team doing His work, I must be His peace broker, introducing His peace formula wherever I find myself.

Making peace. No one would question the need for peacemakers – between nations, within nations, within society, within every social group in society.

Before the peacemaker can tackle the problem, he needs to know what the problem is, *where* the problem is.

Charles Price, Principal of the Capernwray Bible College in Cumbria, is one of the finest British preachers of the last two decades. In the course of his ministry, he is often invited by head teachers into the large comprehensive schools of the north of England.

Standing before a class of 13-14-year-olds he put the question, 'What's wrong with the world?'

There was a forest of hands. Soon the blackboard began to fill up:

People are proud and want to put other people down.

People are jealous.

People are greedy; always wanting what they haven't got . . .

(This was just the start; soon he was faced with a full blackboard.)

Price said, 'OK. That's what's wrong with this world. If we were to stay here after four o'clock this afternoon to consider how to put right what is wrong with the world, do you think we would find anyone here who was proud or jealous or greedy or . . . ?'

The class nodded in assent.

Following some discussion, they decided that what was wrong with the world was also wrong with their school.

Price had another question: 'What if you went home at 4pm and got together your mother, father, brothers and sisters, Grannie, everybody, and said, "The world's in a mess, and our school is just as bad. Let's try to put it right." If you were to stay up all night, do you think, in your family, you might find anybody who was, say, proud, or jealous, or greedy or . . . ?'

The class agreed. There were no dissenters.

It was clear that what was wrong with the world and what was wrong with their school was also wrong with their families.

Price had a final question: 'What if, after school, you climbed a tree and sat there all night trying to decide how to put right what was wrong with the world, would you find any evidence in yourself that you, say, were greedy, or proud, or . . . whatever?'

That was a tougher question. It took some minutes before, often reluctantly, each one nodded a 'Yes'.

Price had his conclusion: 'So what's wrong with the world? I'll tell you what's wrong with the world – You.'

The root of the problem. So how do we put right what's wrong with the world? By sitting on a committee that decides how to impose rightness on the world?

There'll never be peace in the world until there's peace in the hearts of individuals.

The war is over. But in many heads it continues.

The results? As soon as one war ends, another begins. The tensions, the rivalries, the arms races live on. . . .

Between nations and *within* nations, the war goes on. Racism divides societies and sows the seeds of hate which grow into the bitterest of bitter fruits. Management and labour boom out the endless cross-fire of their heavy artillery.

Within nations *and within communities* the war goes on. Greed is born of jealousy and, in turn, begets hate and selfishness with their many unacceptable faces. Alienation breeds contempt for authority and, in turn, *it* begets violence, vandalism, collective neuroses in an infinite variety; and the many faces of crime – all of them unacceptable.

Within communities *and within families* the war goes on. And in no quarter does it rage more fiercely than within the family. Selfishness, the sound of the ominous silence of those who *refuse* to understand, and a total commitment to pleasure divide generations and life partners and so often make the family the opposite of what it was intended to be. It becomes an imprisoning pit of loneliness and frustration. Everyone crying out to be understood. No one prepared to understand. The brisk business of the divorce lawyers, the twisted wrangling over child custody, and those artificial Kramer versus Kramer meetings in the park with Daddy (or Mummy) exercising a legal right to see Johnnie once a week, not knowing what to say to him, being so relieved when the encounter is over: a play for today with all the world a stage and every man, woman and child a player – in need of love, communication, stability, understanding and fulfilment, but finding none of them. The joy of Jesus? Unknown. Conspicuous by its total absence.

The crumbling of the family sends rifts and fissures upwards, downwards, in all directions – and the foundations of society give way.

But even the war within the family is not the most basic of all wars: *There is the war within the individual.* The guilt that saps the mind and stymies fulfilment, the alienation that leaves a wake of loneliness and emptiness and aimlessness: man walking about with a civil war going on in the confines of his cranium. He tries so hard to present a smiling face to the world, but he knows that peace of mind is the pearl that he would pay any price to acquire. But where is the pearl, and can he *buy* it?

The peace formula. 'By his sacrifice (on the Cross, on a green hill, outside Jerusalem, on that spring weekend of AD31 when He opened the way of salvation and joy for sinners, Jesus Christ) . . . made in himself out of the two, Jew and Gentile, one new man, thus producing peace. For he reconciled both to God by the sacrifice of one body on the cross. . . . Then he came and told both you who were far from God and us who were near *that the war was over.'* Ephesians 2:15-17, J. B. Phillips, *The New Testament in Modern English: Schools Edition,* 1960. Italics supplied.

John Stott writes: 'Peacemaking is a divine work. For peace means reconciliation, and God is the author of peace and of reconciliation. Indeed, the very same verb which is used in this beatitude of us is applied by the apostle Paul to what God has done through Christ. Through Christ, God was pleased "to reconcile to himself all things, . . . *making peace* by the blood of his cross."' Colossians 1:20, italics supplied. 'And Christ's purpose was to "create in himself one new man in place of the two (Jew and Gentile), so *making peace*".' Ephesians 2:15, italics supplied.[1]

The war between Jew and Gentile – over. All barriers between man and man – broken down. The battle to *earn* salvation, *deserve* what is beyond our deserts – ended. And all through the free gift of God's grace expressed in the Cross. A gift wide open for all to choose – Jew or Gentile – that out of the two might be made one.

No longer Jew or Gentile – but Christian. No longer bond or free – but Christian. No longer male or female – but Christian. No longer black or white – but Christian. No longer management or labour – but Christian.

No longer nation against nation, class against class, man against man. Even a panacea held out for that unceasing civil war *within* man. All disunity, disharmony, differences, alienations, frustrations, and barriers of separation of all types and descriptions torn down, crushed, dissolved, resolved, abolished – in Jesus.

In Jesus all are gathered into one. One Cause. One Mission. One all-encompassing Purpose. One Voice. One Mind. One Fold. The cause, the mission, the purpose, the voice, the mind – of one Shepherd.

The joy of the peacemaker. Through the Shepherd, all life is not a downward road to disaster, a progress to nowhere, a treadmill to oblivion. It is an upward way to glory. It is hope – live, burning, inextinguishable – in all experiences, through upturn and downturn.

It is love that serves and wins and is catching.

It is a peace that is lasting.

It is unity and reconciliation, oneness.

It is a joy that no man taketh from you.

It is a progress in the family of God to the kingdom of God.

By faith He implants; by hope He imparts; by love He inspires. Christ breaks open the prison of self-satisfaction; invites us to mourn our proud sinfulness, and to allow His Spirit to enter in. The Spirit sends us on limitless adventurings, endless errands of mercy and ministry. And on the road of adventure lie the two pearls beyond our means to purchase:

• *Peace of mind.*
• *The indestructible joy of Jesus.*

The war is over.

It was won at the Cross on a green hill.

Salvation has nothing to do with doing but with what has been done, nothing to do with achievement but with what has been achieved. Blessed Attitudes: the Christian's responses to gift and Giver.

'Even though we were dead in our sins God, who is rich in mercy, because of the great love he had for us, gave us life together with Christ – it is, remember, by grace and not by achievement that you are saved – and has lifted us right out of the old life to take our place with him in Christ in the heavens.' Ephesians 2:4-7, J. B. Phillips, *The New Testament in Modern English: Schools Edition,* 1960.

This is the one way to peace, harmony, satisfaction, fulfilment – and *joy.*

And when the last war is over, the wind-thrashed seas of time stilled, it is the way to eternal life. *Then* sightless eyes will see; the lame man leap as an hart; the tongue of the dumb sing; vacant stares be replaced by the sparkle of reason – and George and Frank will come home.

[1]John Stott, *The Message of the Sermon on the Mount* (IVP 1988), page 50.

UNDERCOVER CHRISTIANS

'Oh the joy of those who are persecuted for the sake of righteousness, because the Kingdom of Heaven is theirs!

'Yours is the joy when men shall heap their insults on you,
and shall persecute you, and shall say in their lies all kinds of
evil things against you for my sake. Your reward will be great in
heaven . . . .'[1]

No one could ever accuse Jesus under the terms of the
Trades Descriptions Act. Right up front He says, 'If you follow
my Way – and make a thorough job of it – expect to be persecuted!'

As soon as you begin to travel the Joy Road, you will
encounter all kinds of difficulties, some big, some little, and
be confronted with all kinds of decisions, some tiny, some
tough.

When I first moved into a particular district, it happened to
be time for an annual door-to-door collection. Out I went with
my red tin. At one door I encountered a man the colour of
whose face matched my tin. In a voice quivering with anger, all
the more unnerving for being quiet, he spat out these words:
'How *dare* you come to my door asking for money? You have
only just moved into the community. I have had Christian
neighbours for twenty years, and they have never as much as
mentioned that they are Christians. I only know because I see
them all piling into a car once a week with Bibles. Now, already,
you're demanding money.' (I almost expected him to add, 'with
menaces'!)

Soon I discovered that his next-door family were members of
the evangelical congregation I attended. At church they were
up-front laity: reading the lesson, playing the organ, organizing
the drinks. Outside the church their Christian affiliation was
kept under wraps, as if covered by the Official Secrets Act.

No one knew. Faced with the option of being thorough-going Christians, and noted for it, they had chosen to become *undercover* Christians.

The phenomenon of the undercover Christian is extremely common in Western Europe, and is one of the main reasons for the decline of Christianity in these countries.

It may be a comfortable arrangement – avoiding pressure points and potential embarrassments – but is flawed and false because Jesus said, 'If you do not acknowledge me before men, I will not acknowledge you before my Father.'

When poverty of spirit has been acknowledged, sins are meant to be mourned and shunned. When meekness 'becomes our inner clothing', we allow the Spirit to direct our lives and, under new management and new direction, changed lives are evidenced in changed attitudes and appetites. When the Christian joins God's peace corps he accepts God's agenda – including the privilege of introducing others to God's Way of peace.

One way or another, it's got to show!

An undercover Christian is a contradiction in terms!

No one is suggesting that, once you stand for the right, the rack and the thumbscrew are round the corner! They don't burn people at Smithfield or outside Balliol College any more, thankfully.

So what about the insults, persecution and slanders Jesus leads us to expect?

First off, let's notice that this happens to us, not because we are insufferable – *and some Christians are!* – but (in the words of Jesus) 'for righteousness' sake' or 'on My account'.

Whatever form persecution takes, it happens because of 'the clash between two irreconcilable value systems'.[2]

And nowhere is the opposition between the value-system of Jesus and the value system of the world more evident than in the Beatitudes!

The 'Blessed Attitudes' of Jesus fly in the face of the world's values and standards.

From the world's perspective, the rich and overbearing are lauded, not the poor in spirit!

From the world's perspective, the careless and laid back have all the plaudits, not those who take sin so seriously they mourn over it!

From the world's angle of vision, the achievers, social climbers and those who trample on the corns and craniums of others to make it to the top receive all the awards, not the meek and the gentle!

As for 'hungering and thirsting after righteousness', where does that come into the How-To-Win-Friends-And-Influence-People credo? When the dealer is faced with an option of Ruthlessness or Righteousness, the clever money is bound to be on the Ruthless every time!

And as for peacemakers; from the world's perspective it rather depends whether peace is politic; I mean, who's winning the war? Is it advantageous to sue for peace?

The pure in heart? Why, they are probably the most ridiculed group of all! Self takes centre stage. And whatever serves self-interest – whatever devious skulduggery makes self come out on top in the scramble – why, that has to be the intelligent option. Right?

That's the recipe for worldly security, popularity, wealth and ease. Right? No persecution down that route, I think.

Perhaps it is because Jesus' Sermon on the Mount so obviously turns the world's values upside down that it has made the nibs so angry! Take Fridrich Nietzsche, for example. His whole life was a violent reaction against his Lutheran background. He set out his principles in a book entitled *The Antichrist* (first published 1895). In his autobiographical sketch, *Ecce Homo*, he represented himself as *the* Antichrist, and revelled in the label!

Nietzsche defines what is 'good' as 'all that heightens the

feeling of power, the will to power, power itself in man'; and what is 'bad' as 'all that proceeds from weakness'. He poses the question, 'What is more harmful than any vice?' and replies, 'Active sympathy for the ill-constituted and weak – Christianity.' Everyone who would be 'strong, brave, masterful and proud' must eliminate from his life the disdainful 'God on the Cross', 'mankind's greatest misfortune'. Nietzsche reserved his commendation for the 'superman' who repudiated the value system of Jesus and used any and every method to climb to the highest position, the ultimate self-made tyrant. Jesus, by contrast, bade His followers be as little children. . . .

Nietzsche, needless to say, was the apostle of Nazism. . . . One man who grasped that from the early stages of the Third Reich was Dietrich Bonhoeffer. A great scholar, he stood up for the cause of Christ when to do so was to take on a totalitarian-state apparatus of a most barbarian kind. He was imprisoned, tortured – and executed by the direct order of Heinrich Himmler in April 1945, days before his concentration camp was liberated by the allies. Bonhoeffer grasped the meaning of the Beatitudes. 'With every beatitude the gulf is widened between the disciples and the people, and their call to come forth from the people becomes increasingly manifest,' he wrote. By inviting the disciples to 'mourn', says Bonhoeffer, Jesus was inciting them to refuse 'to be in tune with the world or to accommodate oneself to its standards . . . '.

And Bonhoeffer was not an isolated example. The twentieth century has been infested with highly technologized totalitarian regimes, Communist and Fascist. That is why it is said that far more Christians have been persecuted – given their lives for the cause of Christ – in the twentieth century than in the previous nineteen centuries combined.

And, depend on it, not one of them has been an undercover Christian.

From the earliest times, the story of Christianity became the story of the persecution of (in the words of the poet) 'the panting, huddled flock whose crime was Christ'. The biblical account provides evidence of the pressure by the Jewish (ecclesiastical) authorities on the Roman (political) authorities to achieve the extirpation of Christianity. History provides the evidence of how, along with the Jews, Christians came to be confronted with the choice 'Caesar or Christ?' – and were impartially, but gruesomely, destroyed. And 'the blood of the martyrs was the seed of the Church . . . '.

Following Constantine's conversion, the distinction between 'ecclesiastical' and 'political' was erased: 'heresy' and 'treason' became the same offence. That was a charter for persecution through the Middle Ages, with its Inquisition, down to Louis XIV and his revocation of the Edict of Nantes.

In an analysis of freedom of conscience across the world in the late twentieth century,[3] Nina Shea, director of Freedom House's Religious Freedom Programme, stated: 'Christians are the most persecuted religious group in the world today, with the greatest number of victims. Increasingly, Christians are harassed, arrested, interrogated, fined, imprisoned and killed because of their religious beliefs and practices.' Three forces are identified as being behind the persecution. First, militant Islamic fundamentalism: Kim Lawton writes, 'Millions of Christians in the Islamic world suffer numerous horrors in virtual anonymity.' Second, resurgent Communism: tens of millions of Christians in China are said to be 'in the midst of the biggest crackdown against Christians in twenty years'. Third, religious nationalism: 'When one religion is used to define national identity, violent clashes may result. Those outside the national and religious norm are accused of betraying their country,' says Jubilee Campaign, a British-based human-rights group. The main offenders are Bulgaria's Orthodox Church, the Roman Catholic Church in many Latin

American countries, and nationalistic Buddhism in Thailand, Sri Lanka and Mongolia.

But the Christian in most Western countries comes up against 'persecution' when his business life conflicts with his principles; when his social life is disrupted by his principles; or when his family life is disrupted by his principles (say, a spouse, a son or a daughter who wishes to pursue a lifestyle hostile to or incompatible with the cause of Christ). No longer is Christianity 'the blood-stained way', but its principles can be inimical to social and economic success and family harmony. And it is these pressures, plus the horror of being 'different', that lead many contemporary Christians to sidestep the joy of Jesus and go 'under cover'.

The existence of the joy of the persecuted will never be doubted by those who have interviewed individuals who have suffered for the cause of Christ, however we may choose to define 'suffer'. When there is a clash between the ideologies of Christ and those of the world, there is also a crucial moment of drama when the Christian takes his stand for the Master, a moment which is crucial in terms of both time and eternity. Paul rejoiced when he could participate in the 'fellowship of his sufferings' (Philippians 3:10). At such a moment, says Jesus, 'Rejoice, and be exceeding glad.'

It is interesting that in the countries where the *real* persecution is occurring, there is no shortage of Christian martyrs. It is in the opulent West where the fear of standing out from the crowd, being 'different', holding fast to principle and facing even the mildest of social pressures has produced the phenomenon of the 'undercover Christian'.

When a 'Christian' does not care enough about Christ to make Him even a topic of conversation, it is likely that in his church-attending habits he is engaged in no more than a social custom. However, many who are shy about their Christian affiliation have not so much a complex about their Christianity as about themselves; 'God can't use me.' In fact, of course, God has never looked for people of great ability to 'use'; just humble people prepared to present themselves to Him as a 'living sacrifice' (see 1 Corinthians 1:26). There is a place for all of us in God's peace corps. There are, of course, just a few people who, although their hearts are filled with Christ, are *genuinely* shy. They can talk about history or steam trains or tall ships, but not Jesus. Behind their condition is a fundamental fear of ridicule which can be overcome only through the power of Christ Himself.

In my teens I went 'under cover' for a couple of years. I broke cover one memorable afternoon in my A-level history class at a College of Further Education. The teacher, a man whom I would willingly have named streets after, had formerly served as a director of education in an African country. There he had encountered Christianity in the form of missionaries. On that memorable afternoon, we were discussing the 'Scramble for Africa'. Suddenly he made a damning statement that struck hard at a large number of conscientious Christians whom I knew; and seemed, at least to me, to strike a blow into the face of Christ Himself. I broke cover. What I said was not, in retrospect, what I should have liked to have said. Clumsily, I had nailed my colours to the mast. There was a sharp intake of breath, not least by the teacher, who was not accustomed to being challenged when airing his atheistic prejudices.

Right there, in front of the class, my Christian convictions were ridiculed and I was asked questions that nothing in my Christian background had prepared me to answer. But answers, of a sort, came.

Religious persecution is never your enemy; and it is often your friend. That proved to be the case in that instance. After class that day I had the first of many 'in depth' discussions with that particular teacher for whom I had the greatest possible respect. When I left college to go to university we kept in touch. After I myself became a teacher, we exchanged Christmas cards and kept up with each other's addresses.

One year, I planned to change my job and wrote to my old history teacher for a reference. The letter he wrote back I shall never forget. It explained that, for some years, he had been suffering from bowel cancer and that during each summer vacation he had been in hospital to have another section of his large bowel removed. In the letter, he made it clear that he knew that he had little time left. And now he had decided to ask the fellow whose faith he had ridiculed some seventeen years earlier to travel to his bedside in Ormskirk, Lancashire, in order to read the Scriptures and say a prayer. When I left his home late one evening, I had the impression that not only was I leaving the home of a *former* atheist but of a thinking man, who, with the maturity of years, had decided that – after all – the cause of Christ was the only way. My joy was indescribable.

[1]Barclay, op cit, volume 1, page 106. [2]Stott, op cit, page 52. [3]*Christianity Today,* 15 July 1996, page 56.

GOD'S SPECIAL THERAPY

Granted, some things in life are tragic. We find others hard to understand, given the limited capacity of the human brain. And some things in life – quite a lot when you keep on the lookout – are positively hilarious.

God went on record to acknowledge the value of the laughter therapy (Proverbs 17:22), and He dispenses His divine medication remarkably frequently. Rather more frequently, in fact, than the customary 'three times a day after meals'! God's medication can ease the hurt of the more painful stuff in life, and put in proportion the menace of the things that threaten.

The Wise Man said, 'There's a time to laugh.' Ecclesiastes 3:4. But it can be a lot more hilarious when it's *not* time. It always seems funnier when humour comes at right-angles to a solemn situation.

I could see it coming! My favourite pianist, Aunty Brenda, always lifts the lid of the church's upright piano so that it hinges back on the other half of the lid.

Now, with most pianists, the deaconess could have stood that over-full vase of dahlias on top of the folded-back piano lid with perfect safety. . . .

But *not* when it was the turn of Aunty Brenda to tickle the ivories! She plays with zest and enthusiasm and, well, *energy*.

From my pew at the back of the large congregation, I watched that vase of dahlias move ever so gradually to the hinge of the folded-back lid.

Eventually, with Aunty Brenda still putting her all into 'Oh! What a glorious sight appears!', there was a loud CLUNK.

The vase of dahlias had fallen among all those strings and little hammers in the innards of the piano. And, though looking around in some perturbation, Aunty Brenda continued to thrash the keyboard. By that time the singing had subsided; the rows of worshippers in front of me were gently heaving in silent laughter. One person near me had a handkerchief stuffed in his mouth. My sister-in-law had told my wife that, if she didn't stop laughing, she would take her out of church and 'smack her legs' (a threat that never worked on the children, either!). An efficient, serious-faced deacon went to the piano, removed the vase and, one by one, the dahlias from the innards. And, when he had finished so had the hymn.

I had given up all pretence at decorum.

A senior evangelical clergyman in the US made a small collection of funny stories in worshipful situations. Ken Holland, a brave editor, agreed to publish them in his magazine.[1] Ken was nearing retirement. Perhaps he was feeling reckless!

At the time when that issue of the magazine appeared, I happened to be suffering from one of my – infrequent – migraines. The title of the article was 'Even the Angels Must Laugh Sometimes!' It caught my wife's attention. She read it in my presence, laughing as quietly as she could in deference to my pounding head. But when she had finished she told me I had to read that article right then! Preposterous suggestion! I couldn't even focus my eyes! An army of little men were using pneumatic drills all over the right half of my brain!

But my wife, named (in the family) after Rider Haggard's heroine 'She Who Must Be Obeyed', insisted.

With a mighty effort I focused on the page and began to read. After a couple of paragraphs I was heaving gently. After a full column I was laughing uproariously. By the time the article finished, I was kicking my heels on the floor.

And there was another thing.

My migraine had completely gone.

I wrote a letter to Ken Holland, congratulating him on his courage in publishing the article. I also asked him for the address of the author, Jan Doward. I was astonished by Ken's reply. Doward's article had provoked an avalanche of mail. Mine was the only letter in favour! Clearly, among the readers of Ken's magazine, the Gift of Joy was in short supply!

I dropped a line to Jan Doward, thanking him for curing my migraine. When he replied a few months later, he told me about his little book titled *Even the Angels Must Laugh Sometimes* (Ferndale House) – and sent me a signed copy. He had made a comprehensive collection of humorous happenings in church and stashed them together in a book. I still enjoy it to this day.

We preachers are an incredibly comical lot. When I study the faces and read the lives of the pulpiteers of yesteryear, I often chuckle. The best of them were – deep down – wild 'n' crazy characters. I'm with Charles Swindoll who said, 'Humour is not making jokes out of life, it's recognizing the ones that are there.'[2]

The laughter that is 'the best medicine' is not provoked by sitcoms, comedians or silly jokes – most are shallow, mindless, prurient and provoke sniggers rather than laughter – but comes from developing a lighter heart through a growing confidence in a loving Lord.

Long ago, a great Christian wrote these words: 'The Christian is joyful, not because he is blind to injustice and suffering, but because he is convinced that these, in the light of the divine sovereignty, are never ultimate. . . . The humour of the Christian is not a way of denying the tears, but rather a way of affirming something which is deeper than tears.'[3]

No doubt, some things in life *are* totally tragic. First among these is a joyless Christian.

Adrian Plass has made a career out of using humour and humorous anecdotes to put points that pack a powerful spiritual punch. Here is part of his version of the Prodigal Son story:

'At last he cometh to his senses and sayeth, "All my father's hired workers have more than they can eat, and here am I about to starve! I will arise and go to my father and say, 'Father, I have sinned against heaven and before thee. I am no longer worthy to be called thy Son; make me as one of thy hired servants.'"

'So he arose and came to his father.

'But when he was still a long way off, his father seeth him and runneth to him and falleth on his neck and pulleth his hair and smacketh his backside and clumpeth him on the ear and sayeth, "Where the devil do you think you've been, Scumbag?"

'And the prodigal replieth, "Father, I have sinned against heaven and before thee. I am no longer worthy to be called thy Son; make me as one of thine hired servants."

'The father sayeth, "Too right I'll make thee as one of my hired servants, Master Dirty-Stop-Out-Inheritance-Spending-Stinker-Pinker-Prodigal! I suppose thou believest that thou canst waltz back in here without so much as an by thine leave, and conneth me with thine dramatic little speech? Thinkest thou that this is 'Little House on the Prairie'? Or mayhap thou reck-oneth that I was born yestere'en? Oh, no. Third assistant bog-cleaner, unpaid, for thee, mine odorous ex-relative."' – Adrian Plass, *The Sacred Diary of Adrian Plass, Christian Speaker Aged 45 3/4* (Harper Collins, 1997), page 117. Republished with the kind permission of the publisher.

Plass recognized that the father, not the 'prodigal son', was the central character of this story. And, for the benefit of those who miss the point of the Jesus version, Plass makes the father's attitude all the more remarkable by turning it upside down! More importantly, even, than that: Plass presents the father in such a way as to reflect the way that most of us prodigals relate to Him, to His character, and to what He has on offer for us.

All parables were told to make a point about God and His kingdom. Too many people, including those who should know better, have a wrong image of God. Or, at the very least, they *behave* as if they have the wrong image.

Jesus said, 'I and the Father are one.'

I never tire of saying: *In God there is no unChristlikeness at all.* If, say, in the Old Testament or in the book of Revelation, you run up against something that suggests to you that God takes a different line from Jesus, then there is something that you have seriously misunderstood.

The character of God is something you've got to get right if you're going to get the most out of your Christian experience.

Adrian Plass is a Christian writer who uses unconventional means to make his points these days. Three centuries ago, his equivalent was John Bunyan.

Both Plass and Bunyan are great on allegories and parables.

Remember Christian in *Pilgrim's Progress*?

Christian's story began in the City of Destruction. As he began to read the Scriptures, two things happened. One, he began to be weighed down by a heavy burden on his back. Two, he realized that he must leave behind that City and all it represented and make for a very different city.

Evangelist gives Christian his directions. But no sooner has he undertaken his trek than he diverges from the beaten track and ends up in the Slough of Despond.

After being helped, dripping mud and bent from his burden, from the slough, Christian encounters Mr Worldly-Wiseman.

Like those who sought to undo the work of the apostle Paul, Worldly-Wiseman believed that salvation was achieved by performance. So he encouraged Christian to make a second diversion from the straight and narrow – to Mount Sinai.

Soon Christian, weighed down by his burden, was toiling up the steep slopes of the mount. The mountain shook and so it was a case of one step up and three steps down. And, all the while, the burden weighed more heavily.

Eventually, Christian gave up the struggle.

At the foot of the mount he again encountered Evangelist. And, for the second time, Evangelist pointed him towards the Cross.

In Bunyan's words, 'Up this way, therefore, did burdened Christian run, but not without difficulty, because of the load on his back. He ran thus till he came to a place somewhat ascending; and upon that place stood a cross, and a little below, a sepulchre.

'So I saw in my dream, that just as Christian came up with the cross, his burden loosed from off his shoulders, and fell from off his back, and began to tumble, and so continued to do, till it came to the mouth of the sepulchre, where it fell in and I saw it no more. Then was Christian glad and lightsome, and said with a merry heart, "He hath given me peace by His sorrow, and life by His death."'

On the level ground at the foot of Calvary's Cross – Christian discovered joy!

Christian was so joyful that he began to dance and sing. His song went like this:

> 'Thus far did I come laden with my sin,
> Nor could aught ease the grief that I was in,
> Till I came hither. What a place is this!
> Must *here* the beginning of my bliss?
> Must *here* the burden fall from off my back?
> Must *here* the strings that bound it to me crack?
> *Blessed Cross! Blessed sepulchre! Blessed, rather be*
> *The Man that there was put to shame for me!*'[4]

Take the points made by Plass and Bunyan together, and you have the twin reasons why some are ensnared by a joyless Christianity, a religion gone bad.

First, too many poor-in-spirit, repentant Christians relate to

God as a hostile tyrant, unable to see Him as the loving Lord, offering unlimited pardon through His unlimited love, a peace that is not manmade but is durable, a joy that is indestructible – and a completely fresh start.

Second, having failed to grasp this Gospel-core, they get hold of the idea that there is a way to heaven from their house via Mount Sinai, spend a large part of their lives clambering up it – then abandon hope.

In the parables of Jesus told in Luke's gospel chapters 14 and 15, we have the Gospel in story form so that, in theory, no one can misunderstand it.

The reward of the saints at the end of all things is characterized as the King's Great Banquet (Luke 14:15-24). The stories of the lost sheep, the lost coin and the lost son (Luke 15) each ends with joy and rejoicing – in earth *and* heaven!

God wants us to enjoy His special therapy: the joy of salvation.

And when just one person latches on to this gift, God's own great heart is so filled with joy that all heaven resounds to the noise of countless millions of beings engaging in joyful celebration.

[1]*These Times,* Southern Publishing Association, Nashville, Tennessee (February 1983). [2]Charles R. Swindoll, *The Final Touch* (Word), page 63. [3]Elton Trueblood. [4]See David Marshall, *An Introduction to the Life and Works of John Bunyan,* Bishopsgate Press (1989), pages 5-13, 31-35.

THE FATHER'S WELCOME

Heaven in party mode; with God cheering the loudest. This is the picture Jesus presents three times as a conclusion to three consecutive stories.

And why the celestial party-giving? Because one lost, solitary earthling has chosen to return to the warmth and light of the Father's presence. (Luke 15:7-10, 25-32.) There may be po-faced Christians, but there is no po-faced God. And the God whose heart is overbrimming with joy and laughter and welcoming warmth, though patient with His po-faced children, finds Himself out of sympathy with them. (Luke 15:22-32.)

This picture of God presented by Jesus was revolutionary. The contemporaries of Jesus believed, 'There is joy in heaven over one sinner who is liquidated before God.' What Jesus said was, 'There is joy in heaven over one sinner who repents.'[1] When a shepherd returned to a Jewish village with a lost sheep across his shoulders, the whole community turned out and there was a great shout of joy and a feast of thanksgiving. That, said Jesus, is exactly what happens whenever a lost earthling returns home to the Father. 'God loves the folk who never stray away; but in His heart there is the joy of joys when one lost one is found and comes home.'[2] Jesus wanted His hearers to understand that it was a thousand times easier to return to the light of the Father's home and the warmth of His heart than to return to the criticism of men. A great Jewish scholar once admitted, albeit reluctantly, that there was one thing that Jesus taught men about God that was absolutely new: that God went out and searched for the lost, and rejoiced when He found them.

The humorous, upside-down picture presented by Adrian Plass of the Father's reception of the Prodigal underlines the real, right-side-up picture presented by Jesus in His story. And that speaks volumes about the generosity and joy of God.

With bullet-proof insensitivity, a younger son had come to his father and said, 'I want my share of the estate now. I'm off.' Why insensitive? It meant he had been wishing his father dead.[3]

The first insight into the father's heart is that, though it was near to breaking, he gave his errant son what he asked for and the freedom to leave for the Far Country.

And in the Far Country the Prodigal felt that life in the bus lane had been exchanged for life in the fast lane. He paced the fastest set in town. He took the substance of life, squandered it – and went bust.

A famine arose; but the famine did not begin on the day the Prodigal's bank balance registered red. It had been there in the background all the time. The economy of the Far Country makes no provision for those who have run through their substance; it has no currency of its own, no welfare system. The law of the jungle prevails. When you've run out of substance, the Far Country says, 'Tough! You want help? No way, no how!'

It is at this stage that the Far Country puts its estimate on prodigal sons and daughters. Doors and purses shut tight. There is no help from anyone. There's a scrapheap in the Far Country for prodigal sons and daughters who've run out of substance.

The Prodigal hit the pits, 'then he came to himself'. Here Jesus, in telling the story, paid mankind the greatest compliment possible. He clearly implied that as long as a man is away from God he is not truly himself, but once he comes to himself and can see things clearly, his impulse is to return to God. Seeing things clearly, the Prodigal knew that his attitude towards his father had been that of a madman; the demands he had made of his father had been the demands of a madman; his behaviour in the Far Country had been the behaviour of a madman.

Strange, though. The inhabitants of the Far Country thought that madness was sanity. Is it possible that they still do? When you leave the Far Country for the Father's house they still shout,

'You're mad!' They have nothing to offer you but the pits, but they tell you you're mad to return to the Father's house.

The Prodigal's decision to return home, as Jesus presents it, was a purely practical one. Even the servants in his father's house were well fed: better be a servant in his father's house than on the scrap heap in the Far Country. But at least he'd learned humility; learned to pronounce the most difficult sentence in any language, 'I have sinned.'

There follows the most heart-warming picture of all; apart from the picture of Christ on the Cross, this has to be the most moving in all of Scripture, *the most productive of joy.* ' "But while he was still a long way off, his father saw him and was filled with compassion for him; he ran to his son, threw his arms around him . . ." ' (Luke 15:20); and then the father didn't give his returning son the opportunity to recite his prepared speech.

The father had never given up on his prodigal son. Day after day his old eyes had scanned the road from the Far Country, peering into every dust cloud for the shape of his returning son. When one day the shape appeared, he barely recognized it: unkempt, haggard, in rags. The scars of sin warp, distort and disfigure. But as soon as the light of recognition came to the father's eye, 'he ran . . . '.

No Eastern father would ever have given that kind of reception to a returning wastrel. Dignified, austere, he would have remained seated, allowing the returning wastrel to grovel. Then he would have decided whether to recognize his existence or not.

Jesus knew all that. That is why He presented the completely revolutionary picture of God the Father running, embracing and kissing the returning boy. I've read that story a thousand times but still that picture gets right in amongst me and stirs me as, I am certain, it has stirred the heart of many a returning prodigal son and daughter down the centuries.

The Prodigal abandoned his prepared speech; he was not given opportunity to fall at his father's feet. Hard hearts cry out, This father was *too* generous! He should at least have demanded a confession!

But the confession of the Prodigal was best made when his head was on his father's shoulder.

God is a fast mover. His love is broader than the measure of men's minds.

It was the attitude of the father that broke the boy's heart and brought him to the point of repentance.

He had come home stinking of the scrap heap; but the father did not demand that he be hosed down. Ignoring the stench, the father placed what John Bunyan called 'the kiss of justification' upon his cheek, consigning his sins to oblivion, lost for ever in the fathomless depths of forgetfulness. The atonement – the Cross – is implicit; and, as far as father and prodigal are concerned, the burden rolls away and is seen no more. There is a great whoop of rejoicing in heaven; the sins of prodigals are lost in the depths of the sea (Micah 7:19).

The lad's prepared speech had said, in effect, Let me make my own atonement. Let my degradation continue. Let me atone for what I have done by what I will do.

But the father would have none of it. He had specific instructions for his servants. 'Bring the best robe and put it on him'; when sins are washed away they are replaced by the robe of Christ's righteousness, woven in the loom of heaven with not a single thread of man's devising.

'Put a ring on his finger'; this symbolized restored authority. 'And sandals on his feet'; this symbolized the acceptance of the Prodigal as a son, not as a slave.

Then, 'Put the fatted calf on gas mark 6, and get ready for a party . . . .' All that the returning Prodigal had been permitted to say of his prepared speech was, 'I have sinned . . . I am no more worthy . . . .' That was enough. That was all that the father was waiting for. The part of the prepared speech that the father's interruption prevented the boy from reciting was his offer to make his own atonement. Jesus meant this to be significant in His telling of the tale; the service of tomorrow can never atone for the sin of today or yesterday. There is no salvation by performance. Our atonement was won by Jesus upon the Cross. The very idea of our seeking to scramble up there with Him is obscene in the extreme.

We are justified by God's grace through faith in Jesus. What is justification? It is a legal verdict the opposite of condemnation. To condemn somebody is to declare him guilty. To justify somebody is to declare that person innocent. When God justifies the sinner, He does not make him righteous; He *declares* him righteous.

This is where some folk get mixed up. They confuse declaring somebody righteous with making him righteous: a legal declaration with a moral transformation. They confuse justification with what comes along with it – sanctification or new birth. Although justification leads to sanctification; although our new status before God leads us to a new behaviour in the sight of God, the two are not to be confused. The foundation of our joy is justification. And we must remember three things about it: our sins are subtracted; Christ's righteousness is added; then God treats us – His prodigal sons and daughters – as if we had never been away from home.

How is justification possible? This is John Stott's answer to this question: 'There is only one ground upon which a righteous God can declare the unrighteous to be righteous, without on the one hand condoning our unrighteousness and on the other hand compromising his righteousness. That ground is the cross of Christ.'

Our sins were nailed to the Cross of Christ. He was our Substitute, our Representative, our Redeemer. In Him our sins receive the condemnation they deserve. Jesus was condemned in order that we might be justified. He was declared guilty that we might be declared righteous. He took our sins to Himself that we might take His righteousness to ourselves.

'Since we have been justified through faith, we have peace with God through our Lord Jesus Christ, through whom we have gained access by faith into this grace in which we now stand. And we rejoice in the hope of the glory of God.' Romans 5:1, 2. The elder brother in the Prodigal Son story was not happy with the whole situation. His face was solemn, angry. And there is something deep within us that comes out in sympathy with him! *By what means* are prodigals justified?

Answer: by faith. Not by performance, track record, achievement, good resolutions, religious devotion: there is no way we can deserve God's justification. We are guilty. We are condemned. We cannot justify ourselves.

We are not justified by 'good works', and faith is not a good work. To be justified by faith does not mean that God rewards our faith by justifying us. To be justified by faith alone is another way of saying that we are justified by Christ alone. Faith has no value in itself. The only value it has is in its object. Christ is the Treasure: faith is only the hand that grasps Him. Christ is the Water of Life: faith is only the mouth that drinks Him. Christ is the Lamb of God slain on the Cross: faith is only the eye that beholds Him. Christ is the Rock of Ages: faith is only the foot that stands upon Him. To say that we are justified by faith alone is to say that we are justified by Christ alone.

But there are elder brothers who will never see this; who will always want to cling to their own works, believing that they can deserve their everlasting inheritance. And, failing to grasp the Gospel, unwashed by the blood of Christ, these elder brothers will be lost.

So the Father does not just want prodigals to repent, but elder brothers, too. That's a tougher assignment. They're already 'in the church', but, unless they realize their poverty of spirit – say with Paul that 'in me dwells no good thing' – they will be lost just as surely as the Prodigal would have been lost if he had never left the Far Country.

The 'Story of the Prodigal Son' is, rightly understood, 'The Story of the Father's Heart'. And that story ends with light shining from every room in the Father's house, and a rumble and shout of rejoicing that can be heard miles away.

Why? In the words of the Father: 'For this son of mine was dead and is alive again; he was lost and is found.' Luke 15:24.

A tremendous picture, that. A picture *and* a prophecy.

The book of Revelation contains a picture of what will happen when God has put an end to time and, by a personal intervention, put an end to sin and made all things new. Included in the picture is a great party, 'the marriage supper of the Lamb'. Present are those who, having turned their backs on the tribulation of earth, have 'washed their robes and made them white in the blood of the Lamb'. They are singing 'a new song' of praise to the One who has saved them. The apostle John, exiled on Patmos by the Roman Empire, saw in vision 'a great multitude that no one could count, from every nation, tribe, people and language, standing before the throne and in front of the Lamb . . . '. Revelation 7:9.

Again there is the rumble and the shout of rejoicing from the Father's house, everyone full of joy. But the road to the joy of this great party had begun at a place of cataclysmic tragedy.

---

[1]William Barclay, *The Daily Study Bible: Luke* (St Andrew Press, 1953), page 207.
[2]Ibid, page 208. [3]One or two commentators have taken a more charitable view towards the younger son. E. A. Armstrong takes the view that a younger son's prospects were bleak and that he was often obliged to take his cut and find his fortune. *The Gospel Parables* (Hodder, 1967), page 170.

THE JOY OF THE JUSTIFIED

'Finally, they came to a place called The Skull. All three were crucified there – Jesus on the centre cross, and the two criminals on either side . . . . ' Luke 23:33, NLT.

Bible translator and Christian martyr William Tyndale said that the Gospel of the Cross was 'good, glad and joyful tidings that makes the heart to sing and the feet to dance'.

In none of the four biblical narratives of the solemn events on Calvary can we find anything that is joyful. Tyndale's comment seems, at best, in bad taste, at worst, almost blasphemous.

How can you use the word *joy* in the same breath as *Calvary?*

Only one Bible writer links the word joy with the Cross: 'Let us fix our eyes on Jesus, the author and perfector of our faith, who for the joy that was set before him endured the cross . . . .' Hebrews 12:2. Here the Cross is viewed as a final humiliation to be endured; an endurance made possible – by the joy of achieving the goal.

What was that goal? The joy of returning to heaven? Or does 'the joy that was set before him' mean more than that? What *was* the goal of Calvary?

The goal of Calvary was its purpose.

On Calvary itself there was no trace of joy. The crown, made of the long-thorned briar, crushed savagely down on the brow of the Prisoner; *'and he sweat, as it were, great droplets of blood'*. The baulk of timber, seven or eight feet long, was borne to the place of execution on the whipped, lacerated back of the Prisoner, this King of Truth, Prince of Peace, 'not of this world'. . . . Roman nails, square in section, were then used to fasten His wrists and feet to that hideous instrument of shame.

Then the Cross, with the Prisoner upon it – *this* Prisoner, *'holy, harmless, undefiled', 'without sin', 'without spot or blemish or any such thing'* – was hoisted in the air and savagely jolted into the manmade socket prepared for it in the rock face. . . . Then the hours of intense, insupportable agony for the Prisoner, no relief from the onslaught on His senses. . . . The tears of John and the women. . . .

Then, at about 3pm, 'Jesus called out with a *loud voice'*. . . . (Luke 23:46, italics supplied.) The writers of the biblical accounts did not find it necessary to explain the significance of the 'loud voice'; their first-century readers were familiar with the facts of crucifixion. No man, except *this* Man, *ever* called out with 'a loud voice' in the last moments before death by crucifixion. He was being asphyxiated. The first readers of the New Testament would understand that the 'loud voice' had a special significance. This was not the weak voice of a man whose life was ebbing away, but the voice of One who yet had all power but who, nevertheless, consented to die, sacrificed Himself, laid down His own life.

And all endured 'for the joy that was set before him': the joy of the goal . . . the joy of making a gateway of joy for sinners.

Isaiah had prophesied it: 'And a highway will be there; it will be called a Way of Holiness. . . . But only the redeemed will walk there. . . . They will enter Zion with singing; everlasting joy will crown their heads. Gladness and joy will overtake them, and sorrow and sighing will flee away.' Isaiah 35:8-10.

From the place of agony, a way of ecstasy. From the place of pain, a way of healing. From the place of humiliation, a way of triumph. From the place of hopelessness, a way of hope, *the* way of hope, *the only* way of hope. From the place where a sinless man died, a way of pardon and victory for sinners. 'Only the redeemed will walk there. . . . Gladness and joy will overtake them. . . . ' *And that way began at Calvary.*

'A highway will be there.' Isaiah's prophetic vision saw the return of the captives from Babylon and Persia to Zion. But did he see further? Did he see other releases from captivity? The breaking of sin's bondage at the Cross and, as a consequence, the return home of many a prodigal son and daughter to a Father with outstretched arms? Did he see an apocalyptic way that would lead to a New Zion, a way of holiness trodden by the redeemed into an eternal City of Joy, joy perpetual and unfading?

The way that begins at Calvary ends in eternity.

The biblical story of King David is outrageous! Those coming to it for the first time invariably feel a sense of outrage that a man with such a record could be forgiven, redeemed. But what made David different from most of the others in the sorry list of the kings of Israel and Judah was that, though he sinned and sinned badly, he never totally let go of God. His relationship with God always meant more to him than his sin.

Psalm 51 speaks volumes about the spiritual experience of King David. 'Have mercy upon me, O God, according to your unfailing love; according to your great compassion blot out my transgressions.' (Verse 1.) The hideousness of his sin cast a sinister shadow over his whole life (verse 3). He acknowledged that his sin had been a stab at the great heart of the Father Himself (verse 4). He longed to be clean again, purged, healed, forgiven. He longed to re-enter God's life of joy, that he might pursue the life of purity (verses 7-9). He freely admitted that only by God's great miracle – a brand-new heart and a brand new spirit – was purity possible in a sinful world (verses 10 and 11). *'Restore to me',* he pleaded, *'the joy of your salvation.'* (Verse 12, italics supplied.) In the period since his great sin what David had missed most through his separation from God was the joy that only God can give.

The way of sin had been a way of sorrow and sadness.

The 'new heart' of God's miracle was the way of joy.

But it was Isaiah in the Old Testament and Paul in the New Testament who explained *how* Calvary was the only means of atonement (at one ment), the gateway to joy.

Isaiah expressed it this way: 'It was our weaknesses he

carried; it was our sorrows that weighed him down. . . . He was wounded and crushed for our sins. He was beaten that we might have peace. He was whipped, and we were healed! . . . And because of what he has experienced, my righteous servant will make it possible for many to be counted righteous, for he will bear their sins.' Isaiah 53:4, 5, 8, 11, NLT.

His hands pierced for the wrong things our hands have done. His feet spiked for the wrong paths our feet have trod. His brow thorn-crushed for the wrong thoughts our minds have harboured. His heart broken that we might have new hearts.

In the New Testament, Paul echoed Isaiah's theology of the atonement.[1] Let one quote suffice as an illustration of Paul's conviction that Christ had died as man's Substitute; 'For God made Christ, who never sinned, to be an offering for our sin, so that we could be made right with God through Christ.' 2 Corinthians 5:21, NLT.

C. H. Spurgeon put it this way: 'The agony was thine, that the ease might be mine. The stripes were thine, that the healing might be mine. The curse was thine, that the blessing might be mine. The crown of thorns was thine, that the crown of glory might be mine. The condemnation was thine, that the justification might be mine.'

The joy of Calvary is the joy of the justified.

The joy of Calvary is the joy of the sinner who accepts the redemption bought so dearly there.

[1]Romans 3:25; 4:24, 25; 1 Corinthians 15:3; 2 Corinthians 5:21; Galatians 1:4; Ephesians 1:7, 8; 5:2; 1 Peter 1:18, 19; 1 John 2:2; 4:10.

ONE MAN'S SEARCH
FOR JOY

Sinners come to the Saviour one at a time, in most cases.

And they come in many different ways.

One of the great Christians of the past century came dragging his heels.

C. S. Lewis, known to his friends and family as Jack, had read books about 'man's search for God'. But, years after he had accepted God's existence, he said that his search had been like 'the mouse's search for the cat'! Accepting God, let alone accepting Christianity, outraged every inclination, prejudice and preconception in this Oxford don.[1]

When the Father set out in search of Jack Lewis, it took Him many years to convince this Prodigal He existed and much longer to lead him home.[2]

Of the night when he 'gave in to God', Lewis wrote: 'I admitted that God was God, and knelt and prayed: perhaps, that night, the most dejected and reluctant convert in all England. . . . The Prodigal Son at least walked home on his own feet. But who can duly adore that Love which will open the high gates to a prodigal who is brought in kicking, struggling, resentful, darting his eyes in every direction for a chance of escape. . . . The hardness of God is kinder than the softness of men, and His compulsion is our liberation.'[3]

The reason for the return to God of *this* Prodigal is of interest here and is not just because he became the twentieth century's most read and listened to defender of Christianity. Nor is it because two major movies – the more recent *Shadowlands* – have been made of his life and spiritual struggle. Nor is it because a tidy number of us were brought up on his Narnia children's books.

Jack Lewis, from an early age, came to see life as the pursuit of an illusive Joy (with a capital J). Commentators on Lewis's work have written that we shall not understand him unless we have a stab at understanding his Joy. They chart the evolution of its meaning through his poems and prose, his books *Pilgrim's Regress* (1932) and *Surprised by Joy* (1955), and his mountains of handwritten notes on the theme of joy.[4]

Lewis's belief that life was about a search for Joy began in his childhood. It pursued him through the hellish boarding schools to which his father sent him. At first Joy meant to him no more than 'an unsatisfied desire which is in itself more desirable than any other satisfaction'. The desire might be fed by a scene or a sunset, or by his adolescent enthusiasm for Norse mythology. Gradually, as an Oxford scholar, Lewis realized that he would know the joy he sought only when he came to know the object of this joy. Only when, aged 33, not on the Damascus road but on the road to Whipsnade Zoo in his brother Warnie's sidecar, did he realize that the object of his search was Jesus Christ and that the Joy he sought was the Joy of Jesus.[5] Lewis remained alone, outside the zoo: 'He felt like a man who, after a long sleep, is now awake.'[6]

The road to Whipsnade Zoo had been a long one. He had abandoned the last vestige of the vague Christianity of his Belfast childhood when he encountered a kindly matron in his prep school, the first of a number of mother substitutes in his life. His own mother's death, which had occurred when he was 9, had devastated him. The youthful, personable matron had involved him 'in the mazes of Theosophy (New Age), Rosicrucianism, Spiritualism, and the whole Anglo-American occult tradition'. He had, however, recognized 'the passion for the occult' as 'a spiritual lust' which 'like the lust of the body has the fatal power of making everything else in the world seem uninteresting while it lasts'. An aspect that attracted him about what he then thought of as 'Higher Thought' was that 'there was nothing to be obeyed, and nothing to be believed except what was either comforting or exciting'.[7]

As he pursued his secondary education, however, he acknowledged that 'authentic joy' had vanished from his life and that pessimism had taken over. He writes: 'Like so many Atheists or Antitheists' he lived in 'a whirl of contradictions. I maintained that God did not exist. I was also very angry with God for not existing. I was equally angry with Him for creating the world.'[8]

As a student at Malvern, he acknowledged that he missed the joy and recalled past experiences when he had felt it. 'To get it again,' he wrote, 'became my constant endeavour . . . .' But his search for joy was in the various areas of his intellectual interest which proved satisfying but not fulfilling joy-wise. As he went up to Oxford, he acknowledged, 'I *should* have realized that, with the fading of interest in Norse mythology, the Object of my joy was further away . . . .' But there was no such acknowledgement.[9]

Lewis came to accept that all his ordinary pleasures were substitutes for joy. He also acknowledged after reading (and meeting) W. B. Yeats that there was no joy to be found in the areas of 'spiritualism, Theosophy and Pantheism'. He came to contrast 'the imaginative longing for joy' with the 'quasi-prurient desire for the occult'. He concluded: 'My best protection (from the Occult) was the known nature of Joy. This ravenous desire to break the bounds, to tear the curtain, to be in the secret, revealed itself more and more clearly the longer I indulged it, to be quite different from the longing that is Joy.' The occult was not only irrelevant to joy; it was, in some sense, an opposite direction.[10]

It was in his fourth year at Oxford that Lewis 'changed scents'. Among the Christian authors who exerted an influence on him were John Milton, Samuel Johnson, John Donne and George Herbert. 'George Herbert . . . was a man who seemed to excel all the authors I had ever read in conveying the very quality of life as we actually live it from moment to moment' but 'the wretched fellow' impregnated all his writing with Christianity. . . .

Following his election as a Fellow of Magdalen College in 1925, Jack Lewis began to speak of God as the 'Adversary' who was tracking him down.[11]

His 'waitings and watchings for joy' preoccupied his mind disproportionately. Then, in 1929, 'There was a transitional moment of delicious uneasiness, and then – instantaneously – the long inhibition was over; the dry desert lay behind.' Joy, he acknowledged, was 'a kind of love . . . turned not to itself but to its object', owing 'its character to its object'. He asked himself if he had been right to desire Joy by itself, rather than the object of Joy. For some time he felt certain that the object was not 'the God of popular religion. . . . Who could have a personal relationship with Him?'[12]

Lewis was selective in giving credit to his colleagues as influences on him in his struggle towards Christ.

He did give credit to 'the hardest boiled of all the atheists I ever knew' (he doesn't name him) who had conceded that 'the evidence for the historicity of the gospels was surprisingly good'.[13] But he was slow to give credit to his close friend Professor J. R. R. Tolkien, a practising Christian, who had long conversations with him. Tolkien provided further proof of the historicity of the gospels and, immediately prior to Lewis's Whipsnade decision, had a long conversation with him which lasted from midnight until four o'clock in the morning.[13]

Lewis himself gives further credit to an unnamed Christian in his circle at Oxford who was 'clearly the most intelligent and best informed man in the class' and who, from Lewis's description, was clearly a Christian of the user-friendly type.[14]

Lewis's conversion, like any genuine conversion, involved an acknowledgement of his sinful nature, his poverty of spirit, his inability to help himself.[15] A central feature was the Person of Jesus Christ. And it was through his encounter with Christ, at the beginning of his personal relationship, that Lewis acknowledged that there at last it was a state of mind which could be described as Joy.[16]

Lewis: the thinking man's prodigal. But the Father's policy towards prodigals takes no account of their intellectual pitch. The Father looks for an awareness of sin and of helplessness. He looks, too, for the sinner's acceptance of the Saviour's provision at Calvary. These, the central conditions of new birth, the Father found in Lewis as in the most run-of-the-mill prodigal. And He welcomed him home.

This leads us to that aspect of Joy that Jack Lewis came to know: the assurance of God's salvation.

[1]C. S. Lewis, *Surprised by Joy* (Collins, 1955), page 182. [2]George Sayer, *Jack: The Life of C. S. Lewis* (Hodder, 1997), page 217. [3]C. S. Lewis, op cit, pages 182, 183. [4]Walter Hooper, *C. S. Lewis: A Companion and Guide* (Harper Collins, 1996), pages 181-193. [5]C. S. Lewis, op cit, pages 20, 61, 106, 134, 135, 137, 142, 143, 165, 175, 176, 178, 184; Hooper, op cit, pages 181, 186, 192. [6]William Griffin, *C. S. Lewis: The Authentic Voice* (Lion, 1986), page 89. [7]C. S. Lewis, op cit, pages 52, 53. [8]Ibid, pages 61, 95 and 134. [9]Ibid, pages 135, 136, 137. [10]Ibid, pages 138, 141-143. [11]Ibid, pages 168, 169, 170, 171, 172. [12]Ibid, pages 173, 175, 176, 178. [13]Ibid, pages 178, 179; George Sayer, op cit, pages 222-225; William Griffin, op cit, pages 65, 66, 88. [14]C. S. Lewis, op cit, page 170. [15]Ibid, page 181. [16]Ibid, pages 188, 190.

FRIENDSHIP WITH JESUS

Whose verdict counts? Pele was a top soccer player in 1967. He was captain of the Brazilian team. He took his team on a world tour. The first stop was an auditorium in Dakar, Senegal. Thousands packed the stands to see the great Brazilian team play a friendly against a local team. Pele said: 'I am determined to do my best so that the people will see some good soccer today.'

Twice in the first ten minutes he received a pass in mid-field. He took the ball down the field, and running right through the defence – they *were* just a local team – he deceived the the the goalkeeper with clever footwork so that he ran out to him. Then, nonchalantly, Pele stepped aside and tapped the ball neatly into the net. *Twice in ten minutes!*

'The second time,' Pele wrote later, 'as I was jogging back to the centre line to restart the game, I saw the goalkeeper waving at the referee. I looked at the goalkeeper. He was sobbing. His heart was broken. I'd never seen a goalkeeper weep before. The referee ran over to him and the man requested to leave the game.'

The substitute came on and the man walked off to the locker room.

'After the match,' wrote Pele, 'I went to find him in the locker room to say, "It's only a game, you know. You were just a local team. You knew you were going to be beaten, didn't you? I was just doing my best. Nothing personal."'

But the man wouldn't see Pele. He was shattered and broken. He believed that the verdict of the crowd was that he was a fool. And he believed that verdict; he accepted that verdict. He thought that Pele's verdict on him was that he was ignorant and foolish, and he believed that verdict, and accepted that verdict.

It broke his heart. Completely crushed him.

People are quick to pass their verdicts on us: 'He's no good!'

'He'll never amount to anything.' 'She's no better than she ought to be.' 'Mediocre at best.' 'Able but idle.' 'A loser.'

Do we have to accept these verdicts?

We're quick to pass verdicts on ourselves; and our verdicts are based on feelings and can be very harsh. Do we have to accept *these* verdicts?

If we do, that's our joy gone for good.

Thankfully, there's only one verdict that counts.

'This is the verdict . . . ' said Jesus (John 3:19).

What is the verdict? And what is the *basis* of the verdict?

We've already considered both the verdict and the basis of the verdict, for, taken together, they are our title to joy. But let's recap:

• The verdict. 'It is by grace you have been saved, through faith – and this not from yourselves, it is the gift of God – not by works, so that no one can boast.' Ephesians 2:8, 9. When Paul Gibson retired as Master of Ridley Hall, Cambridge, a portrait of him was unveiled. At the unveiling, he paid a well-deserved compliment to the artist. In the future, he said, people looking at the picture would not ask, 'Who is that man?' but rather, 'Who painted that portrait?' 'A patient after a major operation is a living testimony to his surgeon's skill, and a condemned man, after a reprieve, to his sovereign's mercy. We are both – exhibits of God's skill and trophies of His grace.'[1]

In Ephesians 2:8, 9 are the three foundation words of Christian joy: salvation, grace and faith. 'Salvation' is more than forgiveness; it is deliverance from death and slavery, and includes the new life in Christ with its new appetites. 'Grace' is God's free and undeserved mercy towards us. 'Faith' is the humble trust with which we reach out and receive grace for ourselves; and it is God's gift; we cannot work it up ourselves.

The credit for the portrait goes entirely to the artist.

The verdict that counts is God's.

• The *basis* of the verdict. 'We implore you on Christ's behalf: Be reconciled to God. God made him who had no sin to be sin for us, so that in him we might become the righteousness of God.' 2 Corinthians 5:20, 21. Christ died the death that we deserve, that we might live the life that He deserves. Therefore, when we accept Christ as our Saviour and Substitute, God, looking at us, sees His Son's perfect life, not our imperfect struggles.

The basis of the verdict that counts? Our attitude towards God's Son, and God's attitude towards His Son.

The verdict is based not on our works but upon Christ's work: Calvary. We are broken, admit our helplessness and, with the outward-thrust empty hand of faith, reach out for the gift of His righteousness.[2]

So whose verdict counts?

Other people's verdicts on us may be important, but not *ultimately* important.

Our verdict on ourselves may influence our behaviour, but it is not *ultimately* important.

Only one verdict is *ultimately* important. And that verdict is God's verdict. It is independent of what other people think of us and what we think of ourselves. Justification by faith says that God has declared us innocent, acceptable, guiltless, without condemnation, 'in Christ Jesus'.

God's assurance, not self-assurance. A couple of years before Isaac Asimov's death, his publishers, Doubleday, reissued his first book *Pebble in the Sky*.

In his first book, Asimov told the story of his parents. They were poor Jewish immigrants who settled in Brooklyn and had to work twenty-four hours a day (almost) to make a living out of a little sweetshop. They saved enough to retire. But when they retired the days seemed empty. So Father got another job and Mother went to night school to learn how to *write* English (she had learned how to *speak* English in the sweetshop!) 'Never too old,' she thought.

Mrs Asimov learned very, very quickly. The teacher said: 'You've done very well, Mrs Asimov. You've learned how to write English. By the way, Mrs Asimov, are you related to the writer Isaac Asimov?'

'Oh yes,' she said, 'I'm Isaac's mother.'

'No *wonder* you learned so quickly! Your son is a great writer!'

Just 4 feet 10 inches tall, Mrs Asimov drew herself up to her full height. She was indignant. 'I beg your pardon! No wonder *he's* such a good writer. He learned from me! I'm his mother!'

She had only just learned to write English but already she had acquired incredible *self*-assurance.

Some people who have studied the Christian Gospel have acquired a similar *self*-assurance. If we are saved independently of our own performance, they have argued, then we can do what we like. One fallacy they have been fond of is 'Once saved always saved'. Out of this misconception has developed the phenomenon of the careless Christian who makes sin a habit of life.

The apostle John had run up against the phenomenon of the careless Christian well before the end of the first century of the Christian era. 'The man who lives "in Christ" does not habitually sin,' wrote the apostle. 'The regular sinner has never seen or known him.' 1 John 3:6, JBP.

The assurance of salvation is essential to the experience of Christian joy, but it is the opposite of *self*-assurance. Self-assurance develops arrogance and pride. Self-assurance has to be destroyed, dissolved, when we acknowledge our poverty of spirit. Not until self-assurance is dissolved can we receive *Christian* assurance: the assurance of God's verdict.

Christian assurance: • The security that comes from knowing

that God accepts you for the sake of Jesus Christ; • And that you really *are* a member of God's family – not just hoping to be, or planning to be.

There is no room for 'once-saved-always-saved'. This belief flies in the face of the most fundamental principle of God's government: freedom of choice. A conversion experience twenty years ago – or even yesterday – does not necessarily mean that you are saved today. It all depends on whether you have the 'in Christ' experience. A justification-by-faith relationship is a day-by-day, ongoing relationship with the Saviour.

Day-by-day with Jesus. What is the secret of maintaining the day-by-day, ongoing relationship with Jesus upon which assurance and joy depend?

On the night of His betrayal, Jesus explained the secret in terms that everyone could understand.

His explanation amounts to the most encouraging revelation to man, apart from the forgiveness of sin. He explained the secret of the life of joy. The Christian is not just a church-going worldling; he has new incentives, new ambitions, new power. He is a new person because he has entered into this new relationship. To use the metaphor employed by Jesus, he has been grafted into the Living Vine – and the life-giving sap of the Spirit flows from the parent stock (Jesus) into the Christian's life.

As Jesus and His disciples walked from the upper room after the Last Supper, down hill to the Brook Kidron and Gethsemane, they were obliged to walk through a number of vineyards.

As was His habit, Jesus explained His truths by drawing on His surroundings.

He began, ' "I am the true vine, and my Father is the gardener. He cuts off every branch that doesn't produce fruit, and he prunes the branches that do bear fruit so that they will produce even more. . . ."' John 15:1, 2, NLT.

Jesus went on to explain that as the 'branch' (the Christian) is integrated with the vine stock (Himself), it bears 'fruit . . . more fruit . . . much fruit'.

The fruit of the Spirit is the spontaneous result of the life-giving sap of the Spirit flowing into our lives. There is no such thing as being a Christian without fruit.

The secret of the Christian life is mentioned ten times in the first ten verses of John 15: 'Abide'. 'Abide in me and I in you.' 'Except a branch abide in the vine . . .' And, if we do not 'abide in the vine'? 'Apart from me you can do nothing.' (Verse 5.) '"Remain in me, and I will remain in you,"' said Jesus. '"No branch can bear fruit by itself; it must remain in the vine. Neither can you bear fruit unless you remain in me."' John 15:4.

So how exactly can we maintain that day-by-day, hour-by-hour, vital connection with the Living Vine? Answer: • Prayer, a two-way communication with God; • Immersion in the thoughts of God through His Word; • Sharing our story and beliefs with others; • The experience of worship and praise.

We will look at them again.

Before we do, I should like you to see just how keen Jesus is for us to have the assurance of His salvation.

---

[1]John Stott, *The Message of Ephesians* (IVP, 1979), page 82. [2]The idea of Christ's death in our place was prefigured by the temple sacrifices in the Old Testament; it was explained in Isaiah 53; and it is to be found, stated and explained, in many places in the New Testament, including Romans 3:25; 4:24, 25; Galatians 1:4; 1 Corinthians 15:3; 2 Corinthians 5:21; Ephesians 5:2; 1 Peter 1:18, 19; 1 John 2:2; 4:10.

THE JOY OF ASSURANCE

Norm's mother died when he was only 3. His father was un-caring and, at times, cruel. Norm's young life was dominated by a sadistic housekeeper.

The result? Norm became a juvenile delinquent. No punishment, however severe, could control him. He felt rejected and, therefore, he behaved badly. He believed that since rejection was inevitably going to result from bad behaviour – then bad behaviour would continue and become worse.

When Norm was 11 his behaviour was notorious throughout the neighbourhood. Other families expressed concern about the way that he and his siblings were treated. The authorities moved in. The day was one he would never forget. The housekeeper had been dismissed for thieving; his father was unaccountably absent and suddenly the living room was filled with police and important-looking people. The children were told that they had been inadequately cared for, and the evidence of that was on their persons and all around them. The authorities had decided that a workhouse or an orphanage would provide a better environment for the remainder of their upbringing.

Just as the family was about to be led away, Norm's father entered the room with a small lady. He soon sized up the situation and began to bluster. Taking his cue from his father, Norm, well built for his age, began to behave abusively towards the representatives of authority.

Suddenly the small lady stepped forward. She announced that that day she and Norm's father had been married. More importantly, eyeing the senior policeman steadily, she announced that from then on *she* would be taking control of that home and responsibility for the behaviour of the children.

It was laughable. And almost everyone laughed, including Norm. The small lady fixed him with a glance and, quite suddenly, he stopped laughing. That was the turning point. The representatives of authority left with the understanding that, for a short period only, they would permit this little lady a time in which she could endeavour to exert control over the hurt and unhappy family.

The little lady had brought into that home love – and Jesus – that day. Both were strangers. She knew that Norm was the real challenge. In the early stages, observers noted little change in his behaviour.

But the little lady was working hard to overcome his feelings of rejection and rebellion. The breakthrough came on the day she announced: 'I don't care what you do; I don't care what you say; it's not in your power to stop me from loving you.'

Norm reeled back in amazement. No one had ever expressed love for him before, let alone unconditional love. Gradually it dawned on him that, no matter what happened, he was still a part of this family and would be unconditionally loved by at least one member of it. His motive for rebellion had gone. What was the point of misbehaviour then? On the odd occasion he tried it he saw tears in his new mother's eyes. He had discovered that disobedience was no longer necessary.

Sometimes we have looked at God in the same way as Norm looked at the authority figures in his early life. We are so sure that God is going to reject us because of what we are that we have kept on being what we are! We have kept on sinning because we have not believed that we have been forgiven. We have remained defeated because we have had no assurance that God accepts us even while we grow.

Does this mean that sin is OK? By no means! When you are unconditionally loved, you do not want to see the hurt in the parent's face or the tears in his eyes. Sin has its consequences – but being rejected by God doesn't happen to be one of them. Not so long as we remain 'in the family', 'in Christ Jesus'. As long as that is the case, we continue to come to Him for healing and forgiveness and power.

The ultimate expression of unconditional love is the Cross. When we have been to the Cross we are, in the words of Thomas Chalmers, 'transformed by the expulsive power of a new affection'. Transformed by love.

Norm's stepmother transformed the family by the power of unconditional love, and especially its most miscreant member.

Norm never looked back. He was my father. I remember him as a man with much warmth and humour in his nature, but no violence. His stepmother died at the age of 98, just nine years before he did. We visited her often and, for a time, she lived with us. My father always treated her with the greatest deference and respect. He was often heard to say, 'She was the best mother *I* ever had.'

But her message of unconditional love is not an easy one to communicate in a world at odds with itself. It is the message of Jesus.

Our assurance of salvation depends upon our relationship with Jesus. It depends upon our continuing to accept His gifts of repentance, and forgiveness, and grace and faith. It depends on keeping that relationship vital and ongoing.

• Jesus said: '"I tell you the truth, whoever hears my word and believes him who sent me has eternal life and will not be condemned; he has crossed over from death to life."' John 5:24. The condition of eternal life is to hear and accept. We must 'believe the Father'. Believe the Father to be, that is, as Jesus presented Him: a God who is love, inviting us all into an intimate relationship in which fear is banished and joy and peace are inbuilt. To believe the Father is to accept the way of life that Jesus offers us – whatever sacrifices may be involved – certain that to accept it is to multiply joy.

• Jesus said, '"My sheep listen to my voice; I know them, and they follow me. I give them eternal life, and they shall never perish; no one can snatch them out of my hand. My father, who has given them to me, is greater than all; no one can snatch them out of my Father's hand. I and the Father are one."' John 10:27-30. Notice, *'I give them eternal life. . . . No one can snatch them out of my hand. . . . No one can snatch them out of my Father's hand.'*

We have to keep on following Jesus; not, like Peter on the night of Gethsemane, 'at a distance' – but close enough to keep our eyes on His face.

By following, we have assurance that no one can snatch us from the security we find in Christ and in God. *Only we can remove ourselves from that security.* It is not God's will that we walk on an insecure tightrope to heaven, unsure as to whether we're going to make it.

The secret, apparently, is to press on. *Press on!* is the title of flying ace Charles Yeager's autobiography. He knew the thrill of breaking sound barriers and lived through enough adventures to sport a chestful of medals. But the message Yeager wanted to pass on to future generations was: *Press on!*

At times, pressing on is quite a challenge. How does the widow press on when the flowers wilt over her husband's grave? How does the victim move beyond the abuse or injustice without turning bitter? How does the patient go on when the Consultant breaks the news about the result of the dreaded biopsy? How does the divorcee press on after the decree absolute? How does anyone press on when the bottom drops out of his or her world?

Part of the secret, as we have discovered, is to abide and, by abiding, draw power to confront the challenge. Part of the secret is to press on – and follow where Jesus leads, trusting Him in situations where there are more questions than answers.

In order to get things sorted out horizontally, we must first square them vertically. Those who rivet on to present misery are invariably those who give up. Remember the vertical dimension: the power of prayer.

• The apostle John wrote a letter of love to congregations divided and quarrelsome and, when he concluded his letter, underlined its purpose and reminded his quarrelsome readers of the truth of assurance: 'I write these things to you who believe in the name of the Son of God so that you may know that you *have* eternal life.' 1 John 5:13.

The knowledge that eternal life has already begun, in itself, provides strength to press on.

• Having expounded the secret of 'abiding in the vine', Jesus said, 'I have spoken these things to you that my joy might be in you, and that your joy might be complete.' The Christian way is a way of joy. And the joy is not just in the goal; it is in the day-by-day journey.

One-hundred-and-thirty-two times in his writings, the apostle Paul uses the expression 'in Christ', 'in Christ Jesus', 'in the Lord'.

The 'in Christ' experience is the substance and secret of joy. To be 'in Christ' is to be as at home in His presence as a bird is at home in the air. To be 'in Christ' is to release our heartaches to Him, knowing that joys multiply when He shares our burden. To be 'in Christ' is to live a life 'hidden with Christ in God' (Colossians 3:3), knowing that Christ is the force, aim and purpose of everything. To be 'in Christ' is to know that our hope for salvation does not depend on a favourable wind or God's being in a good mood. We know that we have the assurance of God's salvation – full and free.

From prison in Rome – death row, awaiting execution – Paul could have written a letter to the Christians in Philippi in which he wallowed in self-pity or, more covertly, invited them to arrange an escape. He did neither of those things. He wrote to the Philippians, urging them to be a people of joy. He told them that what their church needed more than anything else was a joy transfusion.

What's new? A joy transfusion is still the greatest need of the Christian Church.

Pray for a joy transfusion in *your* church – then watch it grow!

The key to Paul's joy was in the 'in Christ' motif: *assurance*. The assurance of salvation is the bedrock joy that made Paul – and can make you – strong in the face of suffering, sin, Caesar and Satan.

As long as we 'abide in the vine', 'are in Christ Jesus', we are – in the words of Paul in Colossians 2:10 – 'complete in Him' – every step of the way. As long as we are 'in Christ Jesus', we are – in the words of Paul in Ephesians 1:6 – 'accepted in the beloved', accepted because of Jesus. As long as we are 'in Christ Jesus', there is – according to Paul in Romans 8:1 – 'therefore now no condemnation'. (KJV.)

God accepts you *as* you are, *not* because of what you are – only for Christ's sake.

He accepts you *just* as you are – but you will not *stay* just as you are; but this is how He accepts you. You don't change first and then He accepts you. He accepts you unchanged, *because* He does not accept you for what you are or for what you will become – but for Jesus Christ's sake.

When the times of struggle come, we would do well to remember the words of Martin Luther: 'If at any stage we look at ourselves we wonder how we could ever be saved. But if at any stage we look at Him we wonder how we could ever be lost.'

At that vital 'moment of acceptance', we are thrown into the heart of the battle. Previously, we have been on the fringes.

Now the arrows fly thick and fast. The other side of the coin is this: we have a panoply, a shield that will resist the fiery darts of the wicked one. Above all, 'we have a Captain who has never lost a battle, and we cannot fail as long as our eyes are upon Him. In Him we have the assurance of God's salvation.'

As long as He is our first love, as long as in Him is our first trust – 'there is therefore now no condemnation for you are in Christ Jesus'.

In the experience of H. G. Spafford, a Chicago lawyer, the truth of assurance was put to the test. He lived in the days of tall sailing ships. His wife and children, including a baby of one year, set sail for Europe. The sailing vessel was called *Le Ville le Havre.*

Mid-Atlantic, in fog, there was a terrible collision. The ship began to go down. Mrs Spafford called her children together for prayer. 'Dear God, save us if you will. Give us the grace to accept whatever happens.'

As the ship sank, her four children were engulfed by the waves. For some considerable period, she held on tight to the baby. But, at last, a wave snatched the child from her grasp. She became unconscious.

When she awoke, Mrs Spafford was on board a vessel bound for Cardiff, having to come to terms with the fact that all her children had been lost. Docking at Cardiff, she telegraphed a message to her husband. He kept that telegraphed message in a frame in his office for the rest of his life: 'Saved alone.'

Spafford immediately caught ship for England. He docked at Liverpool. Mrs Spafford came to meet him. In Liverpool, evangelist Dwight Moody was conducting a tent campaign. He met the Spaffords and was immensely impressed by the faith they showed in the face of the severest adversity *he* could imagine.

Two years later, Moody was staying in the Spafford home in Chicago. He remarked on the fortitude the couple had shown two years earlier. He mentioned that his friend Sankey always wrote a hymn to commemorate great experiences in his life, and encouraged Spafford to do the same. Spafford had never written a hymn before, nor did he write one afterwards. He was influenced by Moody's text for the evening quoting the words of Elisha to the widow: 'Is it well with thee?' And her reply: 'It is well.'

The result was H. G. Spafford's tremendous hymn of assurance:

'When peace, like a river, attendeth my way,
When sorrows, like sea billows, roll;
Whatever my lot, Thou hast taught me to say,
"It is well, it is well with my soul."

'Though Satan should buffet, though trials should come,
Let this blest assurance control,
That Christ hath regarded my helpless estate,
And has shed His own blood for my soul.

'My sin – oh, the bliss of the glorious thought! –
My sin – not in part, but the whole,
Is nailed to His Cross and I bear it no more;
Praise the Lord, praise the Lord, O my soul!

'And, Lord, haste the day when the faith shall be sight,
The clouds be rolled back as a scroll,
The trump shall resound, and the Lord shall descend;
"Even so" – it is well with my soul.'

LOW TIDE AND DARKNESS

'Have you confessed your sin of depression yet?'

For months, Sharon had felt as if she were being, at once, weighed down and suffocated by a heavy, invisible cloud of darkness.

Some years before, Sharon had experienced conversion. Since then she had known joy and assurance, and lived a fulfilled Christian life. At no point had she stopped believing. Her theology of grace was dear to her heart. To impartial observers she appeared like the last word in radiant, out-giving Christianity. . . .

Then the cloud descended.

There was no cause she could identify.

At night she couldn't sleep.

In the daytime she was exhausted and a prey to negative emotions.

She went at her routine of prayer and Bible study as if her survival depended on it. But she felt that her prayers got caught in the attic. And, in a way she was unable to explain, she felt condemned.

She had to force herself to eat.

At first Sharon's husband was understanding, even tackling at the end of a long working day the household chores for which she no longer had the energy. After a couple of months he began to look at her in a strange, quizzical way. Hardness, doubt and cynicism entered his tone. He told Sharon to 'snap out of it'.

It was then that she went to church to be asked by a smug-speaking deacon, 'Have you confessed your sin of depression yet?' And when she told me what happened next – for the first time in her life she made a fist and used it violently – I said, 'Tell me you scored bull's eye!'

I was wrong, of course. I should have had him suspended

from church office and pulled him in for counselling. The fact that I didn't reflected reality. He was vocalising the prejudices of an entire congregation.

In fact, Sharon was suffering from clinical depression.

At this point, examine your own prejudices. If instead of clinical depression I had said bowel cancer or brain tumour, Sharon would have had your instant empathy. But how do you feel about clinical depression?

A friend of mine is a Christian psychiatrist who is married to a clergyman. When he moves, she moves. This means that, more often than is good for her practice, she has to start afresh in a new city.

After one such move, my friend's husband gave her an opportunity to preach in his church. She began with, 'Do you ever get depressed? No, of course, you don't! No Christian ever does! Right?' Suddenly the heads in the congregation began moving back and forth like those of the pigeons in Trafalgar Square.

Right from the time my friend established her practice in that city, she never lacked patients. At first, however, there was not a single Christian among them. Five years later, *all* her patients were Christians, the vast majority from her husband's head-nodding congregation. 'At first,' she observed, 'they told me that Christians did not have emotional or psychological problems. Then, one by one, they came. Christians, after all, had their share of problems of the mind. But those who came had horrendous tales to tell about the intolerance they had encountered in various congregations over the years.'

Why do Christians shoot their wounded?

It would be untrue to say that I have had anything like actual depression. But I would admit to occasional 'low tides'.

I went to school, college and university in towns and cities on the estuary of the same wide river. Nearby, there was a coastal resort with an enormous beach. As a boy I often went to play on it. Had I wanted to diversify my activities to include paddling, I should have had a problem. During the summer months I accepted the existence of the sea by faith alone: the low tides took it miles away. The same low tides were a hazard for the paddle steamer that crossed the estuary. During July and August, unless we timed our crossing carefully, we could spend up to two hours with the vessel stuck on a sandbank. Only the incoming tide would lift the vessel, and enable us to continue our journey.

In my life I've had a number of low-tide, stuck-on-a-sandbank experiences. Perhaps you have. If so, we have put ourselves in the bad books of a whole school of evangelicals who, like Job's comforters, put all problems down to unconfessed sin (Job 4:7, 5, 8). Not to mention, of course, that battalion of flat-feet-on-the-ground-arms-akimbo types who say things like 'Snap out of it!' and 'Get a hold of yourself!'

Did you know that an increasing number of dedicated young ministers are having not just low-tide experiences (however far the tide has gone out, it always comes back), but experiences in which the sea seems to have disappeared permanently, and all they are aware of are the sandbanks? They have been diagnosed as having 'burnout' or 'breakdown' and, in all cases of which I am aware, have been eventually helped back to health.

Are emotional problems limited to ministers? Of course not. When they impact on the laity, the individuals affected, all too often, just slip away quietly.

Or they get shot!

Shot by whom? By arrogant and insensitive clergy and laity.

How are they shot?

People whose emotional problems have resulted in a total inability to control their bodily functions, or meet other people, or eat, or sleep, or get out from under a dark, damp, suffocating cloud that seems to be crushing the very life out of them have been told, 'You've got sin-in-the-life.' *Everyone* has sin-in-the-life. Only One has been perfect. But not everyone has problems of an emotional nature.

We pray for people with cancer, pneumonia and coronary heart disease. How many times have we prayed for people with burnout, depression, or schizophrenia?

What accounts for our attitude towards emotional illness? It's hard for the sighted to appreciate the problems of the partially sighted or the blind. . . .

Recent studies of more than 11,000 cases have verified that depression is more physically and socially disabling than arthritis, diabetes, lung disease, chronic back problems, hypertension and gastrointestinal illness. The only medical problem found to be more disabling than depression is *advanced* coronary heart disease.[1]

Why should I be discussing emotional illness in a book about joy? I'll tell you. Over the years I have met scores of committed Christians who have, at one time or another, suffered from emotional illness. In the great majority of cases, I have observed their being treated inappropriately by Christians who are, for the present, more psychologically robust. And I have to be up front and say that, in the extreme case of clinical depression, the sufferer is no more in a position to 'choose joy' than a cancer victim is to choose instant good health. By contrast, I have known a number of examples of sufferers in the advanced stages of, say, cancer or MS to possess every sign of having the gift of joy! Indeed, the majority of the recipients of that gift, in my experience, have possessed it in spite of, rather than because of, circumstances.

Perhaps this is the right time to say that the joy of Jesus is never triumphalist! It is never insensitive to those for whom joy may be out of reach.

I read this on an American bumper sticker: 'Health and

Prosperity: Your Divine Right'. Always beware of bumper-sticker theology! Always beware of that view of God as a cosmic-fix-it agent who goes ahead of us, dovetailing everything, smoothing out the rough corners and making our lives work like a well-oiled engine. God does not offer that service.

Too many of our prayers are along the lines of, 'Lord, take me out of my circumstances!' And – praise Him! – He sometimes does. But Paul experienced the all-sufficiency of God, not by being removed from his circumstances but by inviting Him into his circumstances, thus transforming them. For years Paul had suffered from a persistent and debilitating illness – migraine? bad eyesight? duodenal ulcers? – but, after having pleaded with God three times to remove it, Paul heard Him say, 'My grace is sufficient for you, Paul, because my strength is made perfect in your weakness.' The weakness was not removed; but Paul was enabled to handle the weakness by seeing clearly that it was God who worked in him and through him.

Some of the greatest Christians have suffered from emotional illnesses.

Martin Luther inspired millions by setting the Gospel right side up with his preaching of 'salvation by grace through faith alone'. But Luther lived through long periods of severe emotional distress. In 1527 he wrote: 'For more than a week I was close to the gates of death and hell. I trembled in all my members. Christ was wholly lost. I was shaken by desperation.' He confessed to being 'subject to recurrent periods of exaltation and depression of spirit.' This oscillation of mood plagued him throughout his life.[2]

Charles Haddon Spurgeon was a great nineteenth-century preacher and teacher of preachers. He communicated joy as few other preachers have. Nevertheless, he once confided to his congregation: 'I am the subject of depressions of spirit so fearful that I hope none of you ever gets to such extremes of wretchedness as I go through.' During these depressions, he said, 'Every mental and spiritual labour . . . had to be carried on under protest of spirit.'[3]

Bible translator, popular preacher and canon of the Church of England, J. B. Phillips, had to cope 'with psychological disturbance' and 'dark depression' on and off for thirty years. In his autobiography he wrote, 'There are times when skies are overcast, when spiritual things seem to have lost their meaning and God Himself appears to be far away. This is where we go to do battle, to go on actively, and even aggressively, believing in the goodness and purpose of God; never mind what happens or what we feel.'[4]

Is it possible that some Bible characters suffered from emotional illness? What was David feeling when he wrote (in Psalm 6), 'I am pining away . . . my bones are dismayed . . . my soul is greatly dismayed . . . I am weary with my sighing'? (NASB.) What was Jeremiah suffering when he wrote, 'I have cried until the tears no longer come. My heart is broken, my spirit poured out. . . . In all the world has there ever been such sorrow?' Lamentations 2:11, 13, NLT.

I'm neither a depressive, nor an expert qualified to treat depression. My aim here is twofold. First, I should like to sensitize you to the existence of depression within the Christian community and to encourage you to treat depressives, and any other sufferers from emotional illness, with the utmost sensitivity and love. As Dwight L. Carlson demonstrates conclusively in his brilliant book *Why do Christians shoot their wounded?* the Christian psychiatrist has a definite role to play. There is no shame in going to Christian counsellors or therapists. Second, I should like to say a few words to those who, like me, experience low tide from time to time.

The tide has, on occasion, returned to lift me off the sandbank when I have • shared my problem, in all its ramifications, with God and with a wise human friend, or, • made a verse-by-verse study of a part of a gospel or one of the letters of Paul (Philippians with its joy theme is a favourite), or, • thought through my problem until I have identified a core, and then actively pursued a course of action – however radical – to remove it, or, • identified the pattern of the tides; an exceptionally low tide frequently follows an exceptionally high tide. . . .

That's how it was with Elijah. The fire had come on Carmel. He had outpaced Ahab's chariot before the rains came. Then, after one nasty letter, within twenty-four hours, he was experiencing low tide in Beersheba. Then, later, an even lower tide at Horeb (1 Kings 18, 19).

Even that joy-hero Paul had his low tides. As first Champion of the Cause of Christ he had preached the Gospel in many cities. He had written down an authentic theology that would still challenge the finest brains twenty centuries later. But, in a letter to friends, he admitted a sandbank situation: 'For we do not want you to be ignorant, brethren, of our trouble which came to us in Asia: that we were burdened beyond measure, above strength, so that we despaired even of life.' 2 Corinthians 1:8, NKJV.

Low tide can follow a spiritual 'high', evangelistic success, a visionary experience – when we are emotionally and physically drained.

Yet, I have come to see my low-tide experiences as being, however traumatic, great learning times, my mind being open to the still small voice of instruction and inspiration. That's how it was for Elijah.

In Isaiah, the central theme is an all-sufficient sovereign Lord with total mastery of the historical process. A century before the Exile began, God, through Isaiah, identified by name the pagan emperor who would bring an end to the exile: Cyrus. For those exiles who would wait anxiously for the arrival of Cyrus on the stage of history – and for all of us who live through dark times in our experiences – God made this promise: 'I will give you the treasures of darkness and riches hidden in secret places, so that you may know that it is I, the Lord, the God of Israel, who calls you by your name.' Isaiah 45:3, NRSV[5]

When dark times come, some Christians react as if, somewhere in Scripture, there is a copper-bottomed guarantee from God that Christians will not encounter trouble – emotional, physical or circumstantial. No such guarantee exists. The guarantee that *does* exist is this: '"Fear not, for I have redeemed you; I have called you by name; you are mine. When you pass through the waters, I will be with you; and when you pass through the rivers, they will not sweep over you. When you walk through the fire, you will not be burned; the flame will not set you ablaze. For I am the Lord, your God, the Holy One of Israel, your Saviour . . . ."' Isaiah 43:1-3.

If we take the two Isaiah texts together, what do they tell us? That bad times will come for God's friends as well as His enemies. That the Christian will, from time to time, be surrounded by threatening circumstances. Fire and water are used in Scripture to denote calamities, 'the latter because it overwhelms; the former because it consumes'.[6] God is saying, bad times, dark times, *will* come. Expect them. Be prepared for them. And *when* they come, this I will guarantee: I will be with you, and My power will be accessible to you; better than that, you will find treasures in darkness, learn the most valuable lessons of life – the *real* gems – in the most unpromising of circumstances.

Remember, on Calvary, *Jesus knew the darkness – the ultimate darkness*. Out of that darkness came His cry: '"My God, my God, why have you forsaken me?"' Matthew 27:46. The records of time and eternity contain no sentence so full of anguish as this one. Jesus had endured the torment of body in silence; but, when it seemed to Him that His Father was a measureless gulf away, His great heart broke.

Please understand this. It's not really death that's the penalty for sin. The penalty for sin is separation from God. Because separation from God is the penalty for sin – Christ had to experience it. On Calvary He was our Substitute: the sin of all ages, of all races of men and women, boys and girls, rested upon Him. He had to know what it was to be forsaken. He could never have taken our place if that had not happened to Him.

We, too, shall know the darkness, but we shall never be forsaken. We may *think* we are, but we are not. Tragedies turn to triumphs. Tunnels have their exits; dark is followed by dawn – and Resurrection Sunday follows Bad Friday – because Jesus lived through the darkness, and conquered it. Note, too, that even in *extremis,* Jesus said, *'My* God.' In the darkest hour He held on. And that is what we must do in those times when we have a great many more questions than answers. Jesus said, 'What I do thou knowest not now; but thou shalt know hereafter.' John 13:7, KJV. Hold on to that when calamity strikes and the dark times come. Jesus has been there before you and, by being there, He has prepared a pathway from ultimate darkness to ultimate light.

Depression and breakdown cannot be described, only discovered. Low tide, by contrast, is at worst a waiting time before God's great love-ocean gives us joy-buoyancy again, and the mighty engine of His Spirit propels us to the harbour of home.

Those living through the trauma of depression may hate me for this final quote. It sounds trite, but it's true. It was inspired by God, but its human author had won the right to commit it to paper by having lived through the valley of the shadow of depression: 'Weeping may linger for the night, but joy comes with the morning.' Psalm 30:5, NRSV.

To those dwelling in the darkness, God makes the promise, 'I will give you the treasures of darkness and riches hidden in secret places, so that you may know that it is I, the Lord, the God of Israel, who called you by your name.' Isaiah 45:3.

[1]K. B. Wells, *inter alia*, 'The Functioning and Wellbeing of Depressed Patients', *Journal of the American Medical Association,* 18 August 1989, pages 914-919. [2]R. H. Bainton, *Here I Stand: A Life of Martin Luther* (Abingdon, 1950), pages 28, 361. [3]Cited, Dwight Carlson, *Why do Christians Shoot their Wounded?* (IVP, 1995), page 39. [4]Ibid, page 40; J. B. Phillips, *The Price of Success: An Autobiography* (Hodder, 1984), pages 196-215. [5]Barry Webb, *The Message of Isaiah* (IVP, 1996), pages 182-184; Edward Young, *The Book of Isaiah* (Eerdmans, 1972), volume 3, pages 197, 198; F. C. Jennings, *Studies in Isaiah* (Loizeaux Brothers, 1935), pages 529-531. [6]Barnes' *Notes on Isaiah,* (Baker Book House), volume 2, page 114.

JOY THIEF NUMBER ONE

Clinical depression is real; it's not the fault of the sufferer; it's not sinful; he can't help himself.

The same is true of other types of emotional illness.

But here I want to make a distinction between *emotional illness* and *state of mind*.

Our attitude to life impacts on our state of mind; that's obvious. Outside the realm of emotional illness, the choices we make and the attitudes we adopt do much to shape our state of mind.

I've known people hanging on to life by a thread or in great pain, to be full of the joy of Jesus.

I've known *Christian* people who, to an outside observer, appear to have everything to be thankful for but who, for one reason or another, feel joy is beyond their reach. At times, I have known people with everything to be grateful for adopting a mournful approach to life only excusable if somebody has just died.

If you're one of those people, or if you have anything to do with one of those people, then this is for you.

Life is a university of hard knocks.

You've noticed!

Me, too.

What counts is how we respond to the knocks when they come – *and* what we learn from them.

Hard knocks are inevitable. Misery as a result of hard knocks is optional. The other option is joy.

When the hard knocks come, it's often useful to ask, What does God want me to learn from this crisis? You will recall that God is the ultimate expert at bringing good out of bad situations. It is not His will that the crises impact on you but, once they do, His close presence is there; His power on tap. He is there to make sure that you come out of the situation ahead of the game. In the darkness, He wants to lead you to the treasure and that treasure you will still possess when the darkness is past.

God has never promised to take us out of our difficulties, to ward off the hard knocks. Sometimes, in His wisdom, He permits us to walk right into them. . . . You doubt that?

Take the time Jesus deliberately permitted the disciples to tumble into trouble. You'll find the story in John 6. Jesus had fed the 5,000. In His country, it got dark around 5.30 to 6pm. It was important to get the crowds home before darkness fell. Hence, Jesus said to His disciples, 'Get into the boat. Cross Galilee. I'll stay here and dismiss the crowds.'

When Jesus gave those instructions, He knew something the disciples did not know: *He knew the weather forecast!*

A number of those disciples were far from being land lubbers. But even seasoned seafarers dreaded those sudden storms that hit Galilee. From Mount Hermon in the north to Sinai in the south there was a deep fissure in the earth's surface. It contained Galilee, the River Jordan and the Dead Sea. When a storm blew up on Hermon, the fissure became a wind tunnel and the height of the waves on Galilee became as threatening as any encountered on the Mediterranean.

The disciples had been in such storms before. On one occasion Jesus had been on board the boat, asleep. The narrative says that the waves were so high they 'came over the boat'. That was the time when Jesus stilled the storm. And He stills some of the storms in *our* lives. But mostly we have to survive those storms with His presence and power a prayer away.

In the post-feeding-of-the-5,000 storm, Jesus left the disciples alone. Indeed, He did not come to them until 'the fourth watch of the night' (between 3 and 6am). Since the narrative makes it clear that the storm began almost as soon as they had put out to sea, and given that they put out to sea before nightfall, we think it is probable that they were left to contend with that storm for between ten and twelve hours.

Then Jesus came to them, walking on the water. Can you imagine Him? The paintings I have seen represent the water as being just a bit choppy. Having been in one of those storms myself, I can assure you that Galilee gets more than choppy! Walking on the water, Jesus would have been way up one minute and way down another. Perhaps it was the fact that He passed in and out of visibility so frequently that caused the disciples to assume that they had seen a ghost. Remember the response of Jesus? If we translate the Greek words literally, the words of Jesus to His disciples read, 'Don't be afraid – because I am'.

Not, 'Don't be afraid – because the storm will blow over in ten minutes.' No, 'Don't be afraid because "I am".' And I AM is the Name of our all-sufficient God.

For once it was Peter who drew the correct conclusion. You can either allow your problems to eclipse the Master, or the Master to eclipse your problems. On this occasion, Peter was from the latter school. He saw that the very element that threatened to be over the disciples' heads, was under the Master's feet. He was walking on the same water that threatened to sink them.

Here's a point worth taking on board. Know why? In Paul's wonderful passage on the consequences of Christ's resurrection (1 Corinthians 15:12-58), he says that *all* hostile forces will be placed 'under His feet' (verse 25). Worth noting, that. There is nothing that threatens to be over your head that is not already under His feet.

Peter looked out through the darkness and the spume and saw visible evidence of the Master's victory. He wanted to join Him! And why not?

Jesus *could* have stilled the storm. He had done it before. But He did not do it on this occasion. *He invited Peter to step into it.*

Notice: • He had permitted the disciples to enter the storm.
• He invited Peter to step into the water.

Why had Jesus done that?

So that the disciples would have an opportunity to discover the complete sufficiency of the Master: that problems do not eclipse the Master, but the Master eclipses the problems.

Christians are not safeguarded from the storms of life. They should, however, be equipped to enter them. In addition, they should trust God to enable them to learn from them.

Paul, above all people, was a man who learned from the crises of life.

Take a dispassionate glance at his story.

He had abandoned a top-flight career to become a Christian. But that had proved to be the beginning, not the ending, of his troubles. The decades of his life that remained to him were filled with persecution and tough times – hard knocks. Few men have been so misunderstood, their motives so misconstrued as Paul. On top of that, you will recall, he had that 'thorn in the flesh': migraine, bad eyesight, whatever.

But Paul never complained, never once wished he had not met Jesus. Once, however, for his own reasons, he listed a few of the problems he had encountered. Take a look at his list: 'Five different times the Jews gave me thirty-nine lashes. Three times I was beaten with rods. Once I was stoned. Three times I was shipwrecked. Once I spent a whole night and a day adrift at sea. I have travelled many weary miles. I have faced danger from flooded rivers and from robbers. I have faced danger from my own people, the Jews, as well as from the Gentiles. I have faced danger in the cities, in the deserts, and on the stormy seas. And I have faced danger from men who claim to be Christians but are not. I have lived with weariness and pain and sleepless nights. Often I have been hungry and thirsty and have gone without food. Often I have shivered with cold, without enough clothing to keep me warm. Then, besides all this,

I have the daily burden of how the churches are getting along.' 2 Corinthians 11:24-28, NLT.

Quite a catalogue, you'll admit.

Was he on a 'poor me' kick? Not on your life! He displayed real embarrassment at having to write in this way (verse 23). So why did he do it? Paul's enemies, who walked in his wake to undo his work, made much of their credentials. They spoke of being a 'chosen people' with an impeccable pedigree. 'So have I,' said Paul, 'but it don't mean a thing!' Then he set out *his* cv, strung out his credentials – *his scars!*

Is Paul encouraging us to parade *our* scars? Certainly not. When we've read about his, we realize that we don't have any worth mentioning. Though from time to time even the most balanced among us get caught up in what computer buffs call a 'feed-forward loop situation'; we get 'stuck in a loop'. When we face difficulties, major or minor, we start compiling a list of them. Then we mull over the list, item by item, find a common theme, and all of a sudden we're at the end of our tether! Item one might have been an annoying encounter; but to that we add all the crises in the family over the past twelve months, half a hundred other irritating encounters, plus the odd full-blown verbal punch-up – and suddenly it's time for that long-scheduled breakdown.

Don't do it! It will ruin your health – and destroy the happiness of those around you.

You have another option. And it's joy!

Anyone can carry his burden, however heavy, for one day. And that's all the Lord asks. Life consists of little things – one step after another, one breath after another, one heartbeat after another, one word after another. Yard by yard, life is hard; but inch by inch, it's a cinch.

When troubles strike – major or minor – you have a choice.

Basically, the choice is between the Jacob way and the Joseph way. Jacob said, 'All these things are against me!' (and

this just prior to his discovery that his son Joseph was still alive
– *and* Prime Minister of Egypt!) Joseph said, 'Man started this
train of events for evil, but God made good come out of it.'

It all comes down to *choice, perspective,* and *trust.*

Choice? My choice of attitudes. My attitude is more important than my past, my education, the contents of my bank
account, my successes or failures. Flashback to chapter two.
It's all there! When my attitudes are right, there's no barrier too
high, no challenge too great.

Perspective? When you add up your problems, they become
too big. When you analyse them, they become too complex.
Dwell on 3am, out-of-proportion, worst-case scenarios – and
they'll crush you. All you are ever required to do is to live one
day at a time. God never gives you more than that with which
you can cope in the compass of a single day. You're designed
to cope with only a dayful of troubles.

Trust? But we're not ever required to cope with today's
troubles alone. Either we do or do not believe in the sovereignty
of God. We *do*? Then let's live as if we do.

Trust God. Ask Him to give you the peace you often forfeit
and take the needless pain you bear. Hand your burdens to the
Lord in prayer. God *is* big enough! Trust is the key.

Self-pity is the greatest joy thief of all. When things happen that
we don't deserve and haven't asked for, our natural tendency is
to curl into the foetal position. It's *natural,* but it helps nobody,
least of all ourselves. Turn it over to God, the Specialist who has
never yet been handed an impossibility He can't handle. Grab
that problem by the throat and thrust it skyward!

Remember Paul's 'famous last words'? His letter to the
church in Philippi? When the Philippians received it, they
probably expected it to be a real rip-snorter! After all, was not
Paul on death row in Rome – daily, hourly – expecting the
arrival of the executioner? Had he not, for some trivial,

trumped-up excuse invented by Jerusalem Jews, been in prison for between five and six years? Years that might well have been the most fruitful of his life?

They may have expected a letter from a man with a chip on his shoulder. What they received was a letter exhorting them to be a people of joy! It had 104 verses and in them no fewer than twenty references to joy.

Yes, Paul admitted that he felt as if his execution had already begun; that he was being poured out like a drink offering (2:17). But hardly had the letter begun when he said, 'In all my prayers for all of you, I always pray with joy.' (1:4.)

It was fourteen years since Paul had first entered Philippi along the Egnation Way. While still in Asia Minor, he had received a vision of a man from Macedonia crying, 'Come over to Macedonia and help us!' And, in response to that Spirit-given vision, there was Paul, in Europe for the first time to conduct his first evangelistic crusade. And Philippi was the chosen location.

First he had brought a career lady called Lydia to Christ. Then, having exorcised a demon from her, he had introduced a slave girl to the Saviour. And then?

It had all seemed to go horribly wrong.

Almost before he knew what was happening, Paul, with his assistant Silas, was being whipped right at the centre of the agora. After that, again with Silas, he was chained by wrists and ankles to a prison wall, his back ribboned and bleeding.

Surely this was time for a pity party? Time for self-pity and bitterness? Time to say, 'Look here, Lord. I was responding to your "Come to Macedonia" vision. Philippi was my first stab at European evangelism. I wouldn't be here but for You. *And look where You have landed me!'*

But that was not how Paul saw it. He exercised *choice* – and his choice was joy! He exercised *perspective* – and saw this was a time of opportunity. He exercised *trust* – and decided to praise

God in song (Acts 16:25). Exactly what happened in heaven that night I have no way of knowing. I have the suspicion that, when God heard Paul and Silas singing, He just said, 'Right, gentlemen! I'm going in!' And as He said it the earth shook round about Macedonia. Paul's chains fell off, but he was free already – because even in the face of being mistreated, thrashed and dumped in a dungeon, he had chosen joy.

Writing his letter to the Philippians in a Roman gaol, he expected no earthquake.

But he was getting on with the business of soul-winning anyway. At Philippi he had led the gaoler and his family to Christ. Then in Rome his witness for Christ had been so powerful among the men chosen to stand guard over him that Christ's Gospel had become 'known throughout the whole imperial guard' (1:12, 13, NRSV) – and there was a congregation of Christians meeting right under Nero's nose (4:22).

In Rome, Paul expected no earthquake to bring him freedom. He had already told Timothy, 'The time of my departure has come.' The battle had been fought, the race won; and the Gospel was triumphant. The prize awaited him (2 Timothy 4:6-8).

But in the time left to him Paul prayed for the Philippians 'with joy'. After all, was this socially and racially diverse bunch of believers – founded by one wealthy woman, one slave girl and one Roman family – not living proof that races, nationalities, social classes and both sexes 'are all one in Christ Jesus'? And, having prayed for them with joy, he exhorted them to be a people of joy (3:1). It is even possible that, in guarded, coded language, he was preparing them to receive the news of his execution with joy (1:27-30).

Will it be self-pity or joy? It will have to be one. It can't be both. They're opposites.

MEGGEZONE CHRISTIANITY: THE JOY-SPOILERS

Journeys to Granny's house were always a great joy. For one thing, a trip on a paddle steamer was involved. For another, Granny paid special attention to children. While the grownups were having lunch at the dining table, Granny had a perfectly scaled-down table and set of chairs for my sister, Audrey, and me, invariably at the younger end of any party. Somehow, that made food a whole lot more appetizing!

Our visits to Granny's place always involved attendance at her church. Before she left after morning service, she would always spare a few moments to chat with 'the old ladies'. (Even the oldest of them was ten years her junior, but we hadn't the heart to point that out!) When I exchanged boyhood for teen-age years, I came to realize why she spared them only a few minutes! Granny's 'old ladies' were as formidable a battalion of joy-spoilers as would ever be discovered inside a Christian church. Don't get me wrong! They knew how to have a good time, sort of. A number of them were great favourites in the local bun fights, parties, socials and whatnots! No. The unattractive aspect of the old ladies was their religion!

The realization that there was such a thing as bad religion first dawned on my mind the day – after morning service – when that formidable battalion of the elderly ran Sister Sweet-Tooth out of town! (All names have been monkeyed with. But the characters mentioned in this story, sadly, *do* bear a resemblance to too many Christians, both living and dead. However, the central characters have all been dead for at least twenty-five years!)

Sister Sweet-Tooth had, as it happens, been a great favourite of mine, and of all the other children. Sister Sweet-Tooth, built somewhat along the lines of the Albert Hall, exuded pure joy. She had a close, intimate relationship with Jesus. Another asset, not without relevance to schoolboys and girls, was that she owned a sweet shop! At the end of the service, Sister S would reach into the deep recesses of her capacious handbag and there would be a small box of liquorice allsorts for each of the children.

Sister S expressed her joy in all kinds of other ways, too; encouraging, building up – and wearing outlandish hats with real flowers in them! A particular vice of the battalion of old ladies was destructive gossip. When they tried to involve Sister S in their lethal talk, she would look confused, then tears would spring to her eyes.

Precisely how they forced Sister S out of the church has never fully been explained to me. Maybe it was her big hats. Maybe it was the sweets. Maybe her non-lethal conversation made the others feel ashamed. Maybe it was the joy they couldn't take. At all events, after divine service one week there were high words. Sister S left in floods of tears and, to my knowledge, she never returned.

Another 'character' in that congregation was Sister E. In my mind E stands for Effort. And Sister E put tremendous effort into her Christianity. In door-to-door collections she raised vast sums of money for the worthiest causes imaginable. Whenever there was work to be done, she was at the head of the queue to do it. Sister E was a lady of considerable intelligence with an excellent grasp of the Scriptures and of Bible doctrine. However, she had a sort of rapid-fire way of talking and, in seconds, could reduce any church attender with the slightest degree of vulnerability to gibbering surrender. She paid particular attention to what the teenage girls were wearing, and hence they absorbed the worst of her invective. For some reason, she seemed to have a soft spot for me!

But, tragically, it was Sister E who took the lead in the running-out-of-town of Sister Sweet-Tooth. However, in doing so, she had the united support of all of her friends, the whole boiling of them!

At Granny's church they had a youth service; and it was in the afternoon. Aware that the younger generation had expressed concern at the Decline and Fall of Sister S, and deducing that part of their motivation might have been selfish, Sister E called the children together at the end of the afternoon service and produced a tinful of 'sweets' out of her handbag. These 'sweets', she assured us, were ones that would be 'good for us'. First she gave one to the pastor, then to each of the boys and girls. I chose a big red one that I thought would be a fruitgum. The pastor almost choked on his and, coughing uncontrollably, made a sharp exit; his 'sweetie' had been a Fisherman's Friend (an extra strong menthyl-based cough sweet used by trawlermen fishing in Icelandic waters!) My friend chose a Zube, and instantly spat it out. My 'fruitgum' turned out to be a Meggezone; my tastebuds took some time to recover!

It seemed to us lads and lasses – and, even now I'm not sure we were altogether wrong – that the contents of the handbags, respectively, of Sister S and Sister E represented, in some mysterious way, an outworking of their – very different – spiritual experiences.

Sister S had the fruit of the Spirit, majoring on joy, and her flavour was sweet.

Sister E majored on 'Do this! Do that!' and hard work – nothing wrong with that! – but added to it condemnation and criticism, and her flavour was tart and bitter. Though well informed and hard working, Sister E did not give evidence of the fruit of the Spirit in her experience, though she did lay claim to one of His gifts: the Gift of Reproof. Sister E was made of the stuff of which martyrs were made. She was articulate, up front – by no means an undercover Christian. She was almost universally admired. But she was not, sad to say, universally loved.

Sister S majored on fruit (though she knew that Christ, not fruit, was the root of her salvation).

Sister E, by contrast, majored on externals – and effort! There was in her nature – as there is in the nature of many of us, imbibed, perhaps with our mother's milk – something that is affronted by the idea that salvation is a free and undeserved gift. Sister E typifies DIY salvation. And who am I to say what her motive was? All I can say is that it appeared that she was attempting to deserve, earn her salvation; and that her very considerable efforts on behalf of the cause of Christ were not, as they should have been, a love response to Christ's sacrifice on Calvary. She never grasped that good works were a consequence, not a cause, of our salvation.

The term that we give to Do It Yourself (DIY) Christianity is *legalism*. Legalism is displayed by those who believe they are saved by keeping the law, in all its ramifications.

Jesus reserved His strongest rebukes for the legalists of His day, the Pharisees. No sooner had Jesus presented His 'Joy Agenda' – the Beatitudes – in His Sermon on the Mount, than He said, 'I tell you that unless your righteousness surpasses that of the Pharisees and the teachers of the law, you will certainly not enter the kingdom of heaven.' Matthew 5:20. To many this would have been a real puzzler. Every Pharisee took a pledge, in front of witnesses, to spend his whole life observing the scribal law in all its detail. The life of the Pharisee centred around law. The Pharisees believed that from the great, wide principles of God's law could be distrained rules and regulations to cover every situation life might present. To distrain those rules and to regulate their living accordingly was their constant aim. Jesus was not opposed to law (Matthew 5:17-19); what He *was* opposed to was law as a means of salvation. The law that began as life ended as legalism, dead and useless as bones in a desert. The Pharisees of the New Testament were obsessed with the trivial, besotted with the molecular: life at ground level.

Furtively, at night, one Pharisee called Nicodemus, perhaps

conscious that something was missing from his life, sought an interview with Jesus. Jesus knew that Nicodemus was great on *theory,* and had come for a *theoretical* discussion. But Jesus saw his need and went straight to first principles. In that area it soon became apparent that Nicodemus, as a typical Pharisee, had not even mastered the alphabet. Jesus told him that what was needed was not a *reformed* man but a *transformed* man. Not a new *leaf,* but a new *life.* Not a life of barren legalism – the righteousness of the Pharisees – but a life rebuilt through the power of God. It was in this context that Jesus said: 'You must be born again.' (See John 3.)

A compulsion had brought Nicodemus to Jesus. And that compulsion was born of the fact that his feet were worn to the bone on the road of legalism. He knew that no matter how hard he tried, he could never deserve salvation. He was right up against the eternal problem: the problem of a man who wants to be changed and who cannot change himself.

Jesus had seen Nicodemus' dilemma from the outset and had come right in with the answers. Nicodemus needed rebuilding from scratch by the Master Builder. Needed to have the motive of law-keeping as a means to salvation replaced by the response of love to the work of the Master Builder. Life at ground level can obscure heavenly perspectives. The rebirth experience needs to happen daily through an ongoing relationship with Jesus who alone can remake us, empower us to live joyfully, and lead us to the City of God.

Jesus reserved His most swingeing attacks for the Pharisees. In the week prior to His crucifixion, He was still doing battle with those miserable hypocrites: '"Woe to you, teachers of the law and Pharisees, you hypocrites! You shut the kingdom of heaven in men's faces. You yourselves do not enter, nor will you let those enter who are trying to.

'"Woe to you, teachers of the law and Pharisees, you hypocrites! You travel over land and sea to win a single convert, and when he becomes one, you make him twice as much a son of hell as you are. . . ."' Matthew 23:13-15.

The legalists were the ones who killed Jesus.

The legalists also plagued Paul. Wherever he went on his evangelistic journeyings he was followed by Judaizers. He presented the case against them in his last book, his letter to the Philippians (3:2-11). And he was obliged to tackle them right at the beginning of his ministry in the letter to the Galatians. Legalism is the oldest Christian heresy.

Did you know that Paul once concluded a letter in large block capitals? He did! And it was Galatians (6:11-18). He draws attention to it. 'See what large letters I use as I write to you with my own hand!' (Verse 11.) Up to this point, Paul had dictated the letter to a secretary. The conclusion of the letter, however, was written in 'large letters' in his 'own hand'.

Why would Paul do that? Was he angry with the Galatians? Not exactly, but he was not exactly pleased with them either (1:6-9; 3:1). Was he short-sighted, his 'thorn in the flesh', perhaps? Very doubtful; the short-sighted do not generally draw attention to their disability. Most Bible students agree that Paul wrote the last eight verses of his letter to the Galatians in his own hand, and in large letters, *for emphasis.*

What was it he was trying to emphasize?

Galatians is the most hard-hitting of all Paul's letters. And that is not too surprising. After all, during his first missionary journey, Paul, with Barnabas, had toiled long and hard to establish churches in the Galatian cities of Pisidian Antioch, Iconium, Lystra and Derbe. The missionaries had received some hard usage, but their evangelism had been blessed by the Holy Spirit. Having evangelized Derbe, Paul would have found it easy to hike through the Silesian gates and go on home to Tarsus. Instead, however, he and Barnabas revisited all four Galatian cities, despite the violence they had encountered, to make absolutely certain that each of the four new churches was thoroughly grounded in the Gospel (Acts 14:21-25).

Imagine Paul's frustration when, after his return to head-quarters in Antioch in Syria, he began to receive disquieting news. Despite his best efforts, the Galatian churches were already beginning to waver in their adherence to the Gospel. The Galatian churches had been 'infiltrated' by 'false brothers' (Galatians 2:4), teaching 'a different gospel' (Galatians 1:6).

It was the substance of this false gospel that led to the Council of Jerusalem. Empowered by the decision of that Council, Paul, from Antioch, wrote to the Galatians. He told them, 'There is no "other gospel", . . . some people . . . are upsetting you and trying to change the gospel of Christ. But even if we or an angel from heaven should preach to you a gospel that is different from the one we preached to you, may he be condemned to hell!' Galatians 1:7, 8, GNB. Strong language!

So what was this false 'other gospel' of the legalists that had thrown the Galatians into confusion?

Paul's authentic Gospel was that salvation is by Christ *plus nothing.* The infiltrators of the Galatian churches had preached a false gospel that amounted to salvation by Christ *plus performance.* For the false Christians, 'performance' began with circumcision, but ended with the need to obey the whole law in every respect in order to achieve salvation, in other words, to make their own atonement (Galatians 5:2, 3). By contrast, freedom was Paul's watchword (5:1). He was not against the law; he *was* against the law as a method to achieve salvation. 'All who rely on observing the law are under a curse. . . . Clearly no one is justified before God by the law, because, "The righteous will live by faith."' Galatians 3:10, 11. 'You who are trying to be justified by law have been alienated from Christ; you have fallen away from grace.' (5:4.)

Paul concluded his letter in capitals, because he was

determined that this time the Galatians would grasp his three central points: • What really counts in the ultimate is *not* behaviour (though that *is* important). • What really counts is *not* our motives (though motives *are* important). • What really counts – the authentic Gospel of Christ as opposed to the false gospel of the infiltrators – is the Cross of Christ.

Of course, the false gospel of the infiltrators was not anything as crude as, 'You are saved entirely by your performance.' The devil is never that obvious! The argument of the infiltrators went something like this: 'Paul's gospel is OK as far as it goes. Our sins are forgiven at the Cross of Christ. BUT – forgiveness of sins speaks only about the past. We're in the present, facing the future. Now we need something more. Not just the forgiveness of sins: what we need now is to be exactly like Jesus. He kept the law to perfection; we must keep the law to perfection.'

In Romans and Corinthians, Paul says that Adam represented the whole human race and that when Adam fell we fell with him. Jesus is the second Adam; and on the Cross He represented the whole human race. When Christ was victorious we were victorious *in Him*. Jesus was 'the second Adam'. But this was the part of the message that the infiltrators could not or would not grasp.

If behaviour (law keeping) is your religion, any religion will do. Because that's what all religions are about: obedience, law keeping, behaviour. But Paul is not interested in *all* religion. He says (Galatians 6:14): 'MAY I NEVER BOAST EXCEPT IN THE CROSS OF OUR LORD JESUS CHRIST, THROUGH WHICH THE WORLD HAS BEEN CRUCIFIED TO ME, AND I TO THE WORLD.'

The 'new creation' (verse 15) is something God has done apart from us. We spoiled the old creation. Ever after that, God, speaking through His prophets, began to promise that there would be a new creation – through Christ. Paul links this new creation with the Cross of Christ. Through the Cross, he says, the world is dead, crucified. What counts is the new world, the new creation.

At the Cross, God judged sinners.

Christ rested in the tomb on the Sabbath.

On the third day He rose from the dead for our justification, filled with new life.

This is the new creation. All who believe in the Lord Jesus Christ are part of that new creation.

What a Gospel!

No wonder Paul used capital letters to write it!

But to the Sister Es of this world, that Gospel will always be too good to be true. In fact, it's too good *not* to be true!

Like the Pharisees who plagued Jesus, and the Judaizers who plagued Paul, Sister E – who has a parallel in every Christian congregation – has surrounded the law with rules and regulations covering every conceivable aspect of life. And these rules and regulations, largely of human invention, as well as the law itself, are used as blunt instruments to inflict sledgehammer blows on first the vulnerable, and, second, those who, like Jesus and Paul, display that peace and joy that so irritate those who do not share them.

The young, in particular, have suffered from the bludgeoning of the modern Pharisees: the joy-spoilers.

Fundamental to the joy of Jesus is the freedom of the Gospel (Galatians 5:1-6). Too many Christians, across the whole spectrum of Christian belief, are bound and shackled by legalists' lists of dos and don'ts, intimidated and immobilized by the joy-spoilers' demands and expectations. And, in all too many cases, the Brother and Sister Es in our congregations vastly outnumber the Brother and Sister Ss.

Wanted! A joy transfusion!

Wanted! Christians who offer a winsome and contagious, sensible and achievable invitation of hope and joy through the sheer power of Christ, and fewer people who project a grim-faced caricature of religion-on-demand.

No one has the right to take the fun out of faith.

The joy-spoilers kill freedom, spontaneity, and creativity. But there is no Christian church or organization without them; no Christian congregation without them. And there is a reason for this. The bad religion of the joy-spoilers is, in some essential sense, the natural religion of the carnal heart. There is a Pharisee in each one of us! Through all the power Christ has made available to you, fight it!

As long as the intolerance of the joy-spoilers is tolerated; as long as the judgemental spirit of the joy-spoilers is unjudged; as long as the bullying tactics of the joy-spoilers continue unchecked; as long as the miserable, narrow-mindedness of the joy-spoilers remains unconfronted – then the Sister Es will always triumph over the Sister Ss, and the church will not grow.

The joy-spoilers have reduced the religion of Jesus Christ to petty rules and regulations, chiefly of their own invention. Their God is too small; their world is too rigid; their lives too unwinsome and their religion too barren.

The Pharisees – joy-spoilers – of this and every other generation have worked on a squeaky-clean exterior. But – and these are the words of Jesus – ' "Inside they are full of greed and self-indulgence" '; not to mention ' "dead men's bones and everything unclean" ' (Matthew 23:25, 27). By contrast, lives transformed by the power of Jesus are transformed from within and, on the outside, display the 'love, joy, peace, patience, kindness, goodness, faithfulness, gentleness and self-control' that are the authentic fruit of a life made new (Galatians 5:22, 23).

The new life offered by Jesus spells joy and freedom; ' " . . . you will know the truth, and the truth will set you free." ' John 8:32.

THE JOY OF FREEDOM

You cannot experience joy in Jesus until you have begun to experience the freedom of Jesus.

Glasnost is a word that entered our vocabulary in the late 1980s. It is Russian for openness. In the early days of glasnost in Russia, the people suddenly became fascinated by history, especially the history of the Stalinist terror. There were blank spaces on just about everyone's family tree, as a result of the millions who had been liquidated during that iniquitous episode. As the full horrors of Stalin's purges became known, one name cropped up again and again: Levranti Beria, chief of NKVD (the grandfather of the KGB).

Beria masterminded the purges in which Stalin's real or imagined enemies were liquidated. If a party official had doubts about the loyalty of a family member, he had only to consult Beria. Beria had files on everybody. He was expert at arranging permanent, discreet 'disappearances'.

Beria, meanwhile, was building up a power base of his own. So great was this power base that he did not have to liquidate his own family embarrassment: his mother. Everyone at NKVD knew that Beria's mother was an ultra-pious Christian. Come Sunday, Beria would send a contingent of secret police to seal off his home town. When the bells of the church atop the steep hill began to ring, the men from NKVD moved in. Beria's mother would emerge from her front door. . . .

She would be on all fours, weeping bitterly. In that way she would progress up the cobbled hill to the church, her knees and hands bleeding, loudly confessing her own sins – and the sins of her wicked son!

From her pitiable outpourings, her neighbours received a picture of a hard, implacable God, as big a horror to Beria's mother as Stalin was to his subjects. By the time she reached the church, bleeding and tearstained, she was in a state of hysteria. Her life had been given to God – but she could not trust Him to save her. She knew nothing of the freedom of the Gospel.

'It is for freedom that Christ has set us free,' wrote Paul to the Galatians. 'Stand firm, then, and do not let yourselves be burdened again by a yoke of slavery.' Galatians 5:1.

Under the tyranny of sin we were slaves. Jesus Christ was our Liberator. Conversion was the act of emancipation. The Christian life is the life of freedom.

The kind of Christianity represented by Beria's mother is more widespread than you might think. Paul wrote Galatians to counter this perverted piety. Previously, Paul had preached to the group of churches in Galatia and won them to the authentic Christian Gospel. But, in his absence, the Judaizers had come along and said, 'Paul's doctrine is dangerous! He is replacing law with licence! Do away with our rules and the church will fall apart! Paul's gospel is all very well BUT you need to add something to it: performance.'

Paul wrote against this error. In Galatians 3:1-25 he posed a riddle: 'Are we saved by performance or promise?' Then he answered the riddle: 'We're saved by the promise of Christ's performance.' Christ's performance – *plus nothing.*

The Pharisees of Christ's time, the Judaizers of Paul's period, and the legalists of our own day are guilty of wielding the subtle power of spiritual abuse. Their long faces and harsh words have scared off many a preacher from teaching the people about the freedom we have in Christ. They have been experts at laying guilt trips on the susceptible, and, by so doing, banishing every bright reflection of joy from their Christianity. They have appointed themselves performance inspectors and quality controllers, dishing out their approval or disapproval, in proportion to an individual's obedience to their rules governing behaviour and appearance.

When Paul spoke of 'freedom' in Galatians chapter 5, he was not speaking of literal freedom; many of the Galatian believers would be slaves. He was using slavery and freedom from slavery to illustrate the spiritual situation of those who'd heard the Gospel.

The Christian, says Paul, lives by faith. In consequence, he experiences the inner discipline of God that is far better than the outer discipline of man-made rules. No man becomes a rebel who depends on God's grace, yields to God's Spirit, lives for others and seeks to glorify God. By contrast, argues Paul, the legalist is the one who eventually rebels because he is living in bondage, depending on the flesh, living for self, and seeking the praise of men and not the glory of God.

Legalism, says Paul, is what is dangerous. It is dangerous because it insists that we make our old natures obey the laws of God. Legalism may succeed for a short time, but then the flesh begins to rebel. By contrast, the surrendered Christian who depends on the power of the Spirit is not *denying* the law of God, nor rebelling against it. Rather, that law is being fulfilled in him through the Spirit (Galatians 5:1-6; Romans 8:1-4).

Christ is our Emancipator. He has set us free from the guilt of sin. In the words of John Stott: 'The Christian freedom Paul describes is freedom of conscience, freedom from the tyranny of the law, the dreadful struggle to keep the law with a view to winning the favour of God. It is the freedom of acceptance with God and of access to God through Christ.'[1]

Paul is not against law (Galatians 5:14; 6:2). He is against using law as a means to justify yourself, to attempt to earn salvation by performance.

There is no salvation in law-keeping. There is no such thing as self-justification, Paul insists. When we try to justify ourselves, he says, we have 'fallen away from grace'. (Galatians 5:4.) Just as with Beria's mother, our religion becomes a misery as, knees bleeding, we seek to struggle up the hill to heaven on all fours.

Since 'Christ has set us free', we must 'stand fast' in the cause of freedom and never submit to slavery again. 'In other words, we are to enjoy the glorious freedom of conscience which Christ has brought us by His forgiveness. We must not lapse into the idea that we have to win our acceptance with God by our own obedience.'[1]

Once we were under the yoke of the law, burdened by its demands and fearful of its condemnation. But Christ met the demands of the law for us. He died for our disobedience and thus bore our condemnation in our place. For this reason we can stand upright and stand firm.

Paul gives a warning. If, like the Judaizers, you set out to achieve salvation by your own effort, you must 'obey the whole law' (Galatians 5:3). And the law is multi-dimensional (see Matthew 5:20-28): it demands not just outward respectability, but perfect feelings, perfect desires, perfect motives, perfect speech – as well as perfect actions! Our only chance of salvation is by surrendering our lives to Christ and, by accepting His sacrifice on our behalf, being covered by the white robe of His perfect righteousness. Our faith must express itself through • acceptance of the perfect righteousness of Christ made possible through Calvary, and • the love response to Calvary which accepts that we owe to God everything that we are, have and can ever hope to be.

The freedom Jesus offers is freedom *from,* freedom *to,* and freedom *in.* • Freedom *from* slavery to sin: Jesus has broken the bonds. • Freedom *to*: Jesus doesn't just want us to give things up (to abandon slavery), but to enjoy a new status as sons and daughters of God – free to love, free to share, free to work together, free to laugh. • Freedom *in* Jesus. 'So if the Son sets you free, you will be free indeed.' John 8:36.

From death row in a Roman prison, Paul wrote to the

Philippians: 'Whatever was to my profit I now consider loss for the sake of Christ. What is more, I consider everything a loss compared to the surpassing greatness of knowing Christ Jesus my Lord, for whose sake I have lost all things. I consider them rubbish, that I may gain Christ and be found in Him, not having a righteousness of my own that comes from the law, but that which is through faith in Christ – the righteousness that comes from God and is by faith. I want to know Christ and the power of his resurrection . . . .' Philippians 3:7-10.

Here is the bottom line of the Christian's experience of joy. Above all things, Paul valued his 'faith-union' with Jesus.[2] Nothing could beat that one-to-one relationship with the Risen Christ: being 'in Christ'. By comparison with that, everything else was a waste of time. Paul had lived with the knowledge of Christ for many years, and had found in Christ an inexhaustible fullness, an inexpressible peace and an indestructible joy. In the same way, the first aim of every Christian is to *know* Christ, 'an ongoing experience which deepens and matures'. To know Christ like this, affirms Paul, is to possess 'the power of God which raised Jesus'.[3]

Paul is saying, Time was when we were hopelessly lost in our lust, helpless to restrain our profanity, our glandular drives, our insatiable greed, our continual selfishness, or our compulsions either to please people or to control and manipulate others. *Then Christ, our Emancipator, came – slavery ended and everything changed.* When God raised Jesus from the dead, He said, in effect, 'No one else need ever live as a victim of sin. All who believe in Jesus Christ, My Son, will have everlasting life and will have the power to live in Me.'

We are free!
We have been emancipated!
What better cause for joy?

In the early days of *glasnost,* freedom was still a novelty in

Russia. It was at that time that a Congress of People's Deputies met. A cab driver from the Ukraine stood up and wagged his finger in the face of Gorbachev – and 150 million people saw him do it on national TV. Gorbachev sat there and took it. Harangued by a cab driver!

A few days later, Gorbachev got up before the same Congress, and one reporter said that he spoke with a voice sly enough to cut paper: 'I'm here to disabuse you people. You think I don't know anything. I know *everything* that is going on. I know about the army veterans who are plotting. I know every word they say against me . . . .'

Gorbachev had proclaimed glasnost, openness; he sat and took it while a cab driver harangued him. Then, on the other hand, he was a man who had come up through the system and, in consequence, knew all about party discipline and authoritarianism.

Before Gorbachev's collapse, observers said that what was going on in his life was going on throughout what was then called the Soviet Union. There were two forces at work: the pull to the West – openness, democracy; the pull to the East – secrecy, authoritarianism.

Gorbachev's struggle was the nation's struggle.

There was a tension in the Church in Paul's day. Paul taught his Gospel of grace and freedom. Then the Judaizers came along and said, 'No. We must go back to the old party disciplines, the old ways, the requirements, the closed society.'

The Christian's life of joy is crushed beneath such a tension.

The authentic life of joy is not lived on all fours, struggling up the hill of salvation, knees and fingers worn to the bone. It is a life lived with your head held high, with your standing tall in the full and complete stature of the Lord Jesus Christ.

[1]John Stott, *The Message of Galatians* (IVP, 1968), page 132. [2]F. F. Bruce, *New International Biblical Commentary: Philippians* (Paternoster Press, 1983, 1989), page 114. [3]Howard Marshall, Epworth Commentaries: *The Epistle to the Philippians* (Epworth Press, 1991), pages 90-92.

THE SECRET OF JOY

'I have learned the secret of being content in any and every situation. . . .' Philippians 4:12. Paul spoke these words from the death cell in Rome. Any day, any moment, the executioner might come calling.

And Paul had been in prison, as a result of an injustice, for between five and six years. He had every reason to feel frustrated and angry.

On his way home from his third missionary journey, Paul had put in at the port of Tyre and spent a week with the Christians there. They had been emphatic: 'For goodness' sake, Paul, don't go to Jerusalem. They plan to kill you!'

When Paul landed at Caesarea and met with the Christians there they were emphatic: 'For goodness' sake, Paul, don't go to Jerusalem. They plan to kill you!'

Up mountain, in Jerusalem, the Christians received him warmly. But, almost certainly, they, too, warned Paul of the plot to kill him.

The crisis came one day as Paul left the temple area. 'The whole city of Jerusalem was in uproar.' While he had been in the temple, the rumour had been spread that he had taken a Gentile into that part of the temple compound exclusive to the Jews. It was untrue; but people with murder in their hearts are rarely fussy about factual accuracy.

Paul had been arrested by the Romans, largely for his own safety. They had not known who he was. While the Jerusalem population were baying for his blood – ' "Away with him!" ' – the commanding officer suddenly discovered that Paul could speak Greek. Surprised, he said, ' "Aren't you the Egyptian who started a revolt and led four thousand terrorists out into the desert some time ago?" ' (Acts 21.)

It is unlikely in the extreme that Paul knew freedom after that arrest – under false pretences – in Jerusalem.

Though a Roman citizen, Paul narrowly escaped whipping. He appeared before the Sanhedrin, and it was soon reduced to uproar. But for the overnight intervention of his nephew, Paul would almost certainly have been murdered by Jews who had taken an oath to do him to death. (Acts chapters 22, 23.)[1]

It took 'a detachment of two hundred soldiers, seventy horsemen and two hundred spearmen' to guard Paul *en route* from Jerusalem back to Caesarea. And even then he had to be moved under cover of darkness. (Acts 23:23.)

Paul was to be imprisoned in Caesarea for two years – AD58-60 – before he appealed to Caesar. (Acts 23:25, 26.) It took eight months – including a shipwreck and a period on Malta – before Paul reached Rome. The book of Acts finishes with Paul under house arrest in the capital of the world 'boldly and without hindrance' preaching 'the kingdom of God'. There, too, Paul remained for two years. (Acts 27, 28. See especially 28:30.)

The book of Acts ends its narrative there. The remainder of Paul's biography has to be pieced together from the autobiographical bites in his letters; and from secular history.

If Nero heard Paul's case at all during this period, it is unlikely that he made any more sense of it than had Governor Festus in Caesarea.

In AD64, Paul's status suddenly changed. Cornelius Tacitus, in his *The Annals of Imperial Rome,* suggests the background of Paul's final months. His status changed from house arrest to being a prisoner in chains. Nero contracted a homosexual marriage and, on the same day, a fire began in the circus adjoining the Palatine and Caelian Hills. The wind fanned it until it lapped at the walls of the mansions, temples and palaces on the Palatine. Soon the noisome, narrow streets were also ablaze. After six days, 'of Rome's fourteen districts, only four remained intact'. And the rumour spread that Nero himself was responsible for the fire. He needed scapegoats, and fast.

According to Tacitus, Nero chose the Christians as his scape-goats. Christianity, Tacitus explained, had been originated by Christ who had been 'executed in the imperial reign of Tiberius by the governor of Judaea, Pontius Pilatus'. Subsequently, Christianity had spread to Rome where it had begun to flourish.

After the fire, records Tacitus, Nero had all 'self-acknowledged Christians arrested'. The majority were killed summarily in the most grisly ways the diseased mind of the Emperor could devise. Some were crucified. Paul, however, was a Roman citizen. And it is likely that he was obliged to face a second – this time farcical – trial.[2]

If Nero had not presided over the first trial he would certainly have presided over this one, if only to ensure its outcome. Before the beheading outside the walls of Rome, Paul had a period of imprisonment, during which he wrote four letters, his second letter addressed to Timothy, his letters to Philemon, the Colossians and the Philippians. In all of these he gave reference to being 'in chains'. In 2 Timothy and Philippians he gave indication of his awareness that his time was running out.[3]

Four times in the first chapter of Philippians, Paul acknowledges his new prisoner status by alluding to being 'in chains'. Nevertheless, it would be impossible to frame a letter in more positive terms than Paul worded the upbeat letter to the Philippians. As he commenced the conclusion of the letter, he said: 'Rejoice in the Lord always. I will say it again: Rejoice!' Philippians 4:4. Paul had lived through many circumstances which must have tested his patience to the extreme, but he had confronted them with joy. (2 Corinthians 11:24-30.)

What is our response to trying circumstances? All too frequently, anger with God, and with anyone else who happens to come within range! We, too, from time to time may feel that we are in a prison. Not one with chains and bars like Paul's prison. But a prison, nevertheless.

It may be a financial prison; if it is, it will be no less real for the fact that we took out our mortgage and signed the papers of our own free will.

It may be that our place of work has become a prison: a dog-eat-dog atmosphere with only the prospect of the weekend to introduce a ray of light.

Perhaps our marriage has become a prison. Or perhaps our sense of loneliness. Perhaps, as we have grown older, our body has become a prison: more and more signs of dysfunction in our aches and pains. Perhaps we live in a prison of unfulfilled dreams: once they told us 'The sky is the limit', now we know that realistically we shall be fortunate to reach the ceiling! Perhaps our prison walls have been built by misunderstanding, injustice and gossip.

If we fall into any of these prison categories, we can, perhaps, in some way identify with Paul. But Paul says, 'I have learned the secret of being content in any and every situation. . . .' And we might be tempted to respond cynically – *'He* doesn't understand what *I* am living through'– except that we are aware that Paul is speaking out of a dark, dismal corner of ancient Rome and has a world of troubles strapped to his back.

What *is* Paul's secret that makes him rejoice even as he faces execution?

The secret Paul expounds – *the secret of the life of joy* – has two aspects:

• In Philippians 4:4-7 he demonstrates how to survive in our inner world – inside our heads – when surrounded by threatening, negative circumstances.

• In verses 10 to 13 he demonstrates how to cope with the circumstances themselves.

The first aspect of Paul's secret . . . . 'The Lord is near. Do not worry about anything . . . .' (Verses 5 and 6, NRSV.) The nearness of God in dark times we have already encountered. But 'Do not worry about anything'? Preposterous, surely! Don't I have the *right* to worry? After all, I was knee deep in bills when I returned from my last trip. Am I not paid to worry about the fate of my family, the company for which I work, the Laodicean state of my local Christian congregation, and the troubles of my church? If my marriage were failing, would it not be irresponsible to do anything other than worry about it? And what about my long-term illness?

Paul's response is unqualified: 'Do not worry about *anything . . . .*'

Paul continues: ' . . . but in everything, by prayer and petition, with thanksgiving, present your request to God.'

What is he saying?

When circumstances arise that worry you, that threaten you, that frighten you – present them to God. Say, 'Lord, I can't face this one alone; I'm running scared – it's bigger than I am. But I present it to You – *with thanksgiving.'*

It's worth noting here that Paul was not thanking God *for* the situation, but *in* the situation. But what, precisely, was he giving thanks for? Just this: the sovereignty of the Lord and the total sufficiency of His love, grace and power. He was saying, 'Lord, the problem is bigger than I am, it frightens me; it came at me out of a clear blue sky – took me by surprise. I give this situation to You, thankful that it doesn't frighten You; it's not bigger than You; it didn't take You by surprise – and I can trust You totally to handle the situation.'

When you've done that, says Paul, in place of panic you'll receive peace. That's the deal. And the peace you receive is 'the peace of God, which transcends all understanding.' And this peace will stand guard over your hearts and minds in Christ Jesus (verse 7).

Some time ago the *Reader's Digest* published a story of a Christian who was suffering all kinds of stress-related illnesses as a result of his business concerns. He came to the end of his tether. In his office he knelt in prayer – and handed the business over to God! That night, the story goes, his peaceful sleep was disturbed by a phone call from the city's fire officer. His factory and warehouses were on fire. The fire officer testified that he had difficulty making the businessman see the seriousness of the situation. Indeed, at first he seemed disinclined to drive to the scene! But eventually he did. There was little left of his business. Someone asked him why he was not more concerned. He replied: 'Yesterday I handed over my business to God. If He wants to burn it down – it's His business!'

An extreme example, perhaps, but it makes the point.

Paul is saying, 'Make a present of those situations that threaten you to God. And in exchange receive His peace. And receive it thankfully; not because you've put your head in the sand, but because He is totally sufficient to handle the most difficult situation, the most threatening circumstances.'

Please notice that Paul is not talking about the God who dissolves our problems, makes life easy and smooths the path before us. The secret he has learned is *not* wanting God to remove him from his situation; rather, he has learned the secret of bringing God *into* his situation.

The life of joy that God offers us is not a life of tranquil, uneventful days, in which He works ahead of us, ensuring that everything nicely comes together. The peace of God is not a peace of tranquillity.

I enjoy making trips to Ireland. Sometimes I fly to Belfast, sometimes to Dublin – always from my local airport. On one of my trips, I looked askance at the plane British Midland had set aside for us. It was like an oblong box with a flat plank fastened to it at right angles by way of a wing. Here I must freely admit that the Short's Sky Van has one of the best safety records of any aeroplane in the world. It's just that it doesn't *look* as if it is capable of taking off and, when it has defied your expectations and ascended above the clouds, it is hard to have that confidence in its ability to stay up there above the Irish Sea that you would like. Perhaps it is for this reason that BM provides such an attractive colour magazine for its passengers – to take their minds off other possibilities.

Trundling over the Irish Sea in the Sky Van, I read about a painting competition run in Irish schools. Each entrant to the competition had to submit a painting with the title 'Peace'. In the issue I read, were reproduced the two prizewinning entries.

The first painting was of the upper lough at Glendalough. The sun was shining; the forested hills were reflected in the clear waters of the lough; and across the centre of the painting was a flight of what looked like Canada geese. The whole picture exuded peace. It was, therefore, with a certain sense of grievance on behalf of the young painter that I noticed that the judges had awarded his painting *second* prize.

The second painting was of the cliffs of Moher, off County Clare on the west coast of Ireland. These must be among the highest cliffs in the British Isles. The whole picture was dark. A storm was in progress and, despite the height of the cliffs, the Atlantic rollers were thunderously smashing against them so that O'Brien's Tower built on the top was awash. Lightning burned through the centre of the picture. The sky was threatening. Only one thin shaft of light came through the black clouds. It illuminated a cleft in the rock. In that cleft was a nest, and on the nest was a gull with unruffled feathers, out of the wind and weather. Underneath it said 'Peace. First prize.'

Whom British Midland chose to judge the competition, I cannot remember. Whoever it was, he knew something about true peace, the peace of God. God's peace is not the peace of an even, tranquil life. It is not a mark of God's blessing when everything's going good and it looks as if God is fixing everything up for us. It is when the breakers are thundering; the wind is howling; and the rain is bashing down that we can find the peace of God. It's the peace that we have when we have handed all our threatening circumstances over to God, with thanksgiving for His total sufficiency. 'And the peace of God, which transcends all understanding, will guard your hearts and your minds in Christ Jesus.'

The second aspect of the secret Paul has learned – the secret of the life of joy – answers the question, 'How do you cope?' Philippians 4:10-13.

'I have learned the secret of being content in any and every situation, whether well fed or hungry, whether living in plenty or in want.' (Verse 12.)

Notice, Paul had 'learned' the secret; it was not instinctive. And, doubtless, his learning process was accomplished as he lived through that litany of injuries, hurts and injustices listed to the Corinthians (2 Corinthians 11:24-30). When the Judaizers had challenged Paul's credentials, asserting the superiority of their own, Paul had said, 'Here are my credentials! Look at my scars!'

But it had all been a learning experience. And what Paul had learned was that God was with him, close by him, in even the worst of circumstances. He did not merely believe that God blessed him only when things were going well. Things rarely did for Paul. From personal experience he knew that, even when stoned and left for dead at Lystra, he could still have the peace and joy of God. That even when, following a shipwreck, he was adrift at sea for a day and a night – the weather rough and the future uncertain – God was so near as almost to be tangible.

Sadly, perhaps even tragically, Christians today have forgotten Paul's lesson. Too many give up on God when negative circumstances strike. Why? Because they have adhered to the false belief that while things were calm and tranquil it was because God was extending to them a kind of favouritism: fixing things, sorting out circumstances, lowering prices, arranging job opportunities and promotion.

It is not only when good things are happening to us that we are in receipt of God's blessings. God's best blessings can be received in the dark, when circumstances are threatening. It is in *these* circumstances that we learn to rely on God, to trust Him, to lean on Him 100 per cent.

Referring to Philippians 4:11-13, Dr Martyn Lloyd-Jones writes, 'Paul sets out in this mighty passage, with its staggering and astounding affirmations, to show the primacy of the Lord and the all-sufficiency of the Lord.' Later he continues: 'There is nothing like the contentment that God gives. If you have that you have everything.'[4]

Paul is harking back to the first principles set out by Jesus; '"Do not worry about tomorrow"' (Matthew 6:34). Do not be over-anxious about the practicalities of food, clothing and anything of that kind. Those who trust in God can have the glorious independence of knowing that He is completely sufficient for their needs. Alluding to this passage, Guy King points back to the Prodigal Son story and the 'bread enough and to spare' that represents our Heavenly Father's resources.[5]

'I have learned to be content. . . . I have learned the secret,' said Paul. So what exactly *is* the secret? Paul expresses it (Phil. 4:13): 'I can do everything with the help of Christ who gives me the strength I need.' (NLT.) What Paul is saying here is that, no matter how threatening his circumstances, he can cope. *How* can he cope? Through the strength of Christ, 100 per cent.

He is saying, 'I can live within my circumstances because Christ is my strength! No matter if I'm well fed or hungry, in a boat in the sunshine – or in a boat that's sinking, I've learned the secret. And the secret is this: "Jesus Christ is my strength and, that being the case, He is proof against any threat and more than equal to any situation."'

Paul had talked about many situations, good and bad, and then concluded: he had the strength to cope with any kind of situation because of the Person who gave him the power.

F. F. Bruce says it like this: 'It was, indeed, when he (Paul) was most conscious of personal weakness that he was most conscious of the power of Christ resting on him.'[6] Elsewhere, Paul stated, 'I will boast all the more gladly about my weaknesses, so that Christ's power may rest on me. That is why, for Christ's sake, I delight in weaknesses, in insults, in hardships, in persecutions, in difficulties. For when I am weak, then I am strong.' 2 Corinthians 12:8-10.

Alluding to the difficulties he had confronted when evangelizing in Asia, Paul wrote: 'We are hard pressed on every side, but not crushed; perplexed, but not in despair; persecuted, but not abandoned; struck down, but not destroyed.' 2 Corinthians 4:8, 9.

Hard pressed, persecuted, perplexed: that's life! But never crushed, never in despair, never destroyed – *because never abandoned*. Why? 'We always carry around in our body the death of Jesus, so that the life of Jesus may also be revealed in our body.' (Verse 10.)

Paul is insistent that the work he has done is not his own work but the work of God. William Barclay expounds: 'It is God who has made him adequate for the task which was his. It may be that he is thinking of a fanciful meaning that the Jews sometimes gave to one of the great titles of God. God was called *El Shaddai*, which is The Almighty, but sometimes the Jews explained *El Shaddai* to mean *The Sufficient One*. It is he who is all-sufficient who has made Paul sufficient for the task.'[7] And who can make us sufficient for any task.

What is important about you and about your Christian service is nothing in yourself, your persona, your judgement, your talents. Jesus Christ is your life, your strength.

Charles Price told this story at the Christian Booksellers' Convention in 1997.

The owner of a Christian bookshop had reached his late 80s. He had known fat years and thin. When the bad times came he had a saying: 'For this I have Jesus.' He had it printed on bookmarks and, over the years, sold many hundreds of them.

In 1995 that man had a stroke. Price phoned his wife. Her husband had just returned home from hospital. She explained that it was unlikely that Price would be able to understand his speech since, as a result of the paralysis, it was badly slurred. Charles Price opened the conversation with the words, 'I'm so sorry to hear that – '. That was as far as he got. For Price found that he understood exactly what the old bookshop owner was saying: *'For this I have Jesus. No matter what the situation, I have Jesus. Jesus is my strength.'*

Price had been much moved by this incident. A few weeks later he used it as an illustration at the Keswick Convention. A woman had attempted, without success, to make contact with him. A few days later she wrote to him in these words: 'Two years ago my husband was killed in a road accident. We had two children and this was the most tragic thing that could ever happen to our family. The day before he was killed a friend of mind wrote to me and enclosed with the letter a little bookmark with the words, "For this I have Jesus." I looked at it and thought, "That's nice", and put it down on the kitchen table. Then the policeman came to my door and told me that my husband had been involved in an accident and that I must go and identify his body. When I arrived home, there on the kitchen table was the bookmark, "For this I have Jesus".' The woman continued her letter: 'I cannot tell you what that has meant to me these last two years: For this I have Jesus. So much so, that we have had it inscribed on his tombstone: For this we have Jesus.'

Here is the foundation of the Christian's joy, the Christian's peace and the Christian Gospel: the Person of the All-sufficient Lord.

Despite this, the substance of much of Christian prayer is, 'Lord, change my circumstances; take me out of my circumstances . . . .' And, praise God, He sometimes does!

But the secret Paul had learned was not for God to take him out of the situation, but to bring God into the situation – *and discover His total sufficiency.*

It is in times of darkness, menace and crisis, when things get tough, that we learn the secret of joy: total trust, total dependence on the all-sufficient Saviour.

Graham Kendrick heard the 'For this we have Jesus' story at the Keswick Convention and was inspired to write these lines:

> 'FOR THE JOYS AND FOR THE SORROWS –
> the best and worst of times,
> for this moment, for tomorrow,
> for all that lies behind;
> fears that crowd around me,
> for the failure of my plans,
> for the dreams of all I hope
> to be, the truth of what I am:
>
> *'For this I have Jesus.*
>
> 'For the tears that flow in secret,
> in the broken times,
> for the moments of elation,
> or the troubled mind;
> for all the disappointments,
> or the sting of old regrets –
> all my prayers and longings,
> that seem unanswered yet:
>
> *'For this I have Jesus.*
>
> 'For the weakness of my body,
> the burdens of each day,

for the nights of doubt and worry
when sleep has fled away;
needing reassurance
and the will to start again –
a steely-eyed endurance,
the strength to fight and win:

'For this we have Jesus.'
– Graham Kendrick.[8]

[1]See David Marshall, *Footprints of Paul* (Autumn House, 1995), pages 106-138.
[2]Marshall, op cit, pages 128-138; J. B. Lightfoot, *The Crossway Classic Commentaries: Philippians* (Crossway Books, 1994), pages 21-29. [3]2 Timothy 4:6-8; Philippians 1:19-21, 23-24, 27, 29; 2:17. See Colossians 4:3, 18; Philemon 10, 13. [4]M. Lloyd-Jones, *The Life of Peace,* (Hodder, 1993), pages 204, 206. [5]Guy H. King, *Joy Way: An Expositional Study of Philippians* (CLC, 1984), page 115. [6]F. F. Bruce, *New International Biblical Commentary: Philippians* (Paternoster Press, 1983, 1989), pages 150-151. [7]William Barclay, *Daily Study Commentaries: Corinthians* (St Andrew Press, 1954), page 210. [8]Graham Kendrick © 1994 *Make Way Music,* PO Box 263, Croydon, Surrey, CR9 5AP, UK. International copyright secured. All rights reserved. Used by permission.

JOY EXPLOSION

'If the fire that worked in Paul and in the Philippian church worked in us, then we could face anything that might come.'
Dr Martyn Lloyd-Jones, *The Life of Joy* (Hodder, 1993), page 14.

How can that happen?

We must experience the person and power of Jesus in our own lives. Remember Paul's aim above all aims: 'I want to know Christ and the power of his resurrection.' Philippians 3:10.

Society tries to drive our efforts by offering us impressive trophies: silver platters, bronze plaques, gold medals. We like recognition. But what does it do? It drives us to strive for more recognition! Universities give scholarships and prizes. Companies give bonuses and gold watches. The world of athletics gives medals. And, in the scribbling business, there's always the Pulitzer Prize. But, in the words of the old cliché, do any of them 'give happiness at the personal level'?

The trouble is, the high-achiever mentality transfers itself into the spiritual realm. We try to earn Brownie points from God! We look for signs that our strivings have earned God's nod of approval! Paul had taken this view until he encountered Christ outside Damascus. He then knew that his old drive for DIY righteousness and earthly applause was, at best, seriously misguided. Instead of scoring 100, he felt he scored zero. And all those honours? 'Rubbish.' Having clothed himself in the pride of self-achievement, he now stood stark naked and spiritually bankrupt.

Paul started to live – *really* live – when he encountered the person and power of the Risen Saviour.

After that, Paul was no longer driven by confidence in performance but by a consuming passion to spend the balance of his years knowing Jesus more intimately, drawing upon His resurrection power more increasingly, entering into His sufferings more personally and being transformed into His image more completely. His dreams of making it all on his own were for ever dashed on the solid rock of Christ Jesus.

Are *you* one of the high achievers? If so, these are the things that will count in your world: • Your position/title. • Your monthly salary and perks. • Your popularity with your peers. • The awards hung on your walls. • The size, make and type of your car. • A wardrobe full of elegant clothes in the latest fashion. • A big house in the pucka part of town. • Your chances of climbing higher. • Your sense of power in knowing that you can buy whatever you want whenever you like. • The feeling of accomplishment – you did it!

If that's you, then you're a member of that elite club: MITTT – *Made It To The Top.*

If that's you, then take a look at another list: • What about satisfaction at the personal level? • What about your personal life? The real you, when nobody's looking? Contented and at peace? • Your marriage? Your relationship with your children? Everything OK in that department? • What about the essential you? Still scared and insecure? Any habits out of control?

Check your priorities by running through these questions: • What if you contracted a long-term illness, perhaps a terminal one? • What if you lost your earning power overnight? • Are you ready to die? • Are there secrets that haunt you? • Are there paralysing worries and insecurities that won't quit, regardless of how much money you've got? • Has all the fun gone out of your life? Do you laugh (I mean *really* laugh) now that you have 'arrived'? Or are you too driven to relax?

Try to answer those questions honestly.

Paul's point in Philippians 3 is that spending your life trusting in your own achievements brings you glory but leaves you spiritually bankrupt. He invites you to stop right here, to look at

Christ's accomplishment on the Cross, to give Him the glory – and to invite Him to provide you with His perfect righteousness for ever.

It worked for Saul of Tarsus. It turned him round completely. You'd never have heard of him if it hadn't happened.

You need to know Jesus – His person and His power.

Trouble between man and man begins with troubles *within* man. The man who argues with himself generally wants to argue with someone else. Get right with God, and the rest follows. Sooner or later we shall all be in a prison of one sort or another – grief, illness, alienation, loneliness – and, before that happens, we need to learn the secret of how to live in the joy of Jesus, regardless of the circumstances. That way we rise above them, rejoice in tribulation, and become conquerors.

❏ Saved to serve, we need to be salt to a decayng society and light to a darkening world. We can neither be salt nor light if we do not have a daily, even hourly, live link with the Lord. Only by maintaining the vital connection with the living Vine can we bear fruit and experience the joy of Jesus to overflowing (see John 15:1-11, NLT). Without that vital connection – through prayer, the Word and worship – there is no assurance, only anxiety (see John 5:24; 10:27-30). 'A Christian is not so much an advocate, but a witness, and this witness is not effective without assurance.[1]

Seventy years after John saw Jesus in the flesh, he was still excited about the experience. 'That which was from the beginning, which we have *heard,* which we have *seen* with our eyes, which we have *looked at* and our hands have *touched* – this we proclaim concerning the Word of life. The life appeared; we have seen it and testified to it, and we proclaim to you the eternal life, which was with the Father and has appeared to us. . . . *We write this to make our joy complete.*' 1 John 1:1-4, italics supplied.

Notice whose joy was made complete by the privilege of witnessing for the Risen Saviour: *'Our* joy'.

❏ Grasp the glorious Gospel of Christ, believe it, live it and, if necessary as with Paul in Galatians, be prepared to do battle for it. 'What is offered to us by this Gospel is not something contingent; it is an absolute offer. The Gospel of Jesus Christ promises to the man who truly loves and believes it that whatever his circumstances and his condition, and whatever anyone else may do, his joy can and shall abide.'[2]

Allen Redpath once said, 'When God wants to do an impossible task, He takes an impossible man and crushes him.' Paul was such a man: strong willed, stubborn. That's why he had to be crushed. Had to be brought to the point where he 'counted as rubbish' all his achievements 'for the sake of Christ'. It was at the point when Paul realized the glorious Gospel of Christ – that his salvation depended upon Christ's righteousness, not his own – that he began to experience joy, perhaps for the first time in his life.

Today the entire Church needs to receive the joy transfusion that Paul received at this point in his experience. It is the key to revival. It is the key to growth. It is the key to maturity.

There's a lot of long-faced, heavy-hearted stuff in Christian worship these days. And, as a consequence, worship itself is joyless and hard to hack. Church is the one place where life's burdens should be lighter, attitudes uplifting and positive; but, more often than not, joy is curbed by the spiritually 'superior' faces, the worship 'quality controllers' – evaluating everything in terms of how *they* think it ought to be – and the usual priggish puritans.

When the Philippians read Paul's letter, they received a joy transfusion. If Paul – given what lay ahead of him and what he was suffering at the time – could be full of joy, then so could anybody. Was there a secret clue to Paul's joy? The assurance of salvation? His capacity for trust in God? That is certainly borne out by the narrative of his life. Regardless of his situation, Paul invariably took the view that God was still the sovereign director of his life and that he, Paul, need not concern himself about it. To Paul, God was not a distant deity but a constant reality.

❑ Battle self and subdue it: that is the message of the second chapter of Philippians. 'Let the same mind be in you that was in Christ Jesus, who, though he was in the form of God, did not regard equality with God as something to be exploited, *but emptied himself,* taking the form of a slave, being born in human likeness. And being found in human form, he humbled himself and became obedient to the point of death – even death on a cross.' Philippians 2:5-8, NRSV, italics supplied.

We live in an era of self-promotion. But Christ *emptied Himself.* We stick up for our rights, take care of ourselves first, win by treading on other people's corns (and craniums), achieve by intimidation, push for first place and have a store of other self-serving agendas. *And that attitude does more to squelch our joy than any other.*

Greece said: 'Be wise, know yourself.'

Rome said: 'Be strong, discipline yourself.'

Religion said: 'Be good, conform yourself.'

Education said: 'Be resourceful, expand yourself.'

Psychology said: 'Be confident, assert yourself.'

Materialism said: 'Be possessive, please yourself.'

Humanism said: 'Be capable, believe in yourself.'

Pride said: 'Be superior, promote yourself.'

Christ said: 'Be unselfish, humble yourself.'

In our selfish, grab-all-you-can society, the message of Christ is you will not get anywhere joy-wise until, first and foremost, you acknowledge your poverty of spirit, your complete inability to help yourself.

Philippians chapter 2 verses 5-8 was an early Christian

hymn. Paul used it to illustrate to the Philippians that, in becoming human, Christ was the ultimate in submission. His aim? To co-operate with God's plan of salvation. He did not lobby for His right to remain in heaven; He did not picket for the benefit of His exalted role. He agreed to a plan that would require His releasing ecstasy and accepting agony. In a state of absolute perfection and undiminished deity, Jesus willingly came to earth. He left the adoration of angels, unselfishly accepting His role as one that would require His being misunderstood, abused, cursed and crucified. He unhesitatingly surrendered the protection of the Father's glory for the lonely path of obedience and agonizing death.

The result? 'God exalted him to the highest place and gave him the name that is above every name, that at the name of Jesus every knee should bow . . . and every tongue confess that Jesus Christ is Lord.' Philippians 2:9-11.

All knees must ultimately bow before the crucified Saviour. On earth there is no higher place than at the foot of His Cross. It is as we kneel there that He releases His joy in our lives.

❑ United *with* Christ, we must be united *in* Christ – pulling together, like minded – and thus make His joy complete (Philippians 2:1-3). 'Do everything without complaining or arguing . . . .' (2:14.)

The Greek words Paul uses here translate as 'grumbling' and 'disputing'.

Some years ago I stood where Luther stood when he defended himself at the Diet of Worms. The imposing hall – long since destroyed – had been crammed with princes, landgraves, margraves, dukes and electors of the German Empire, Emperor Charles V in the chair. They were there to rule on one German monk's declaration of belief in salvation by grace alone.

Nerves were taut like piano wire. But Luther stood alone,

unintimidated and resolute. Just before his audience with the Emperor, the princes and the prelates, a friend had come alongside the maverick monk and asked, 'Brother Martin, are you afraid?' Luther responded: 'Greater than the Pope and and all his cardinals, I fear most that great pope, *self*.'

And so should we. It knocks life out of kilter, shoves us into patterns of negative thinking – and makes us grumblers and grousers. In the Roman prison, Paul felt that his life was already being poured out, but declared, 'I am glad and rejoice with all of you. So you too should be glad and rejoice with me.' (2:17, 18.)

Paul was scarred, but not calloused. On the point of being done to death, but not discouraged. Here is the acid proof: *The joy of Jesus really is indestructible – and proof against all circumstances!*

❑ We must keep our eyes on the goal – heaven – and on our Mentor – Jesus Christ.

Paul tells us to be imitators of Christ; but it's only human to look to human mentors. Every human mentor I ever had proved, sooner or later, to be a disappointment. I have never been disappointed in Jesus. We live surrounded by enemies of the Cross (Philippians 3:18, 19). So many, in fact, it made Paul weep. He provided the clearest, most pointed description of a person who is lost. He or she is: • destined for eternal hopelessness; • driven by sensual appetites; • dedicated to material things. These things can drown the sound of laughter and kill the feeling of joy.

We belong with those who are bound for heaven; our citizenship is there (Philippians 3:20, 21); 'the Jerusalem that is above is free', and we belong there – not on this passing planet (Galatians 4:25, 26). So, 'Rejoice in the Lord always. I will say it again: Rejoice!'

❏ That great preacher Dr Martyn Lloyd-Jones spent the concluding years of his fruitful ministry praying for and preaching revival: Joy in the Holy Spirit. Revival is something that committees cannot organize; celebrations cannot duplicate and we cannot work up. Only God can send it down.

The revival spoken of in Scripture, said Dr Martyn, was not something confined to preachers or leaders or notable persons; it was to be the experience of 'ordinary people'.[3] At Pentecost, Peter had said, ' "The promise is for you and your children and for all who are afar off – for all whom the Lord our God will call." ' Acts 2:39. And that is very comprehensive!

Dr Martyn had studied both the Scriptures and the history of revivals. Of this he was certain: 'The next manifestation . . . is the element of joy and gladness. Here is something that you find running through the New Testament.' 'The inevitable result', he continues, of grasping the Gospel of justification by faith is, first, 'assurance' and, second, 'great joy'. Peter had called this joy 'a joy unspeakable and full of glory'. 1 Peter 1:8, KJV.

Before His ascension our Lord had promised 'a full joy, an abounding, abundant joy' 'and he had promised it in connection with his sending of the Holy Spirit'.[4]

The apocalyptic portions of Scripture indicate that the Second Coming of Jesus Christ will occur when 'this gospel of the kingdom will be preached in the whole world as a testimony to all nations' (Matthew 24:14), after the Holy Spirit has descended upon the Church in Latter Rain outpouring and following 'a great tribulation' (Mark 13:24, KJV; Revelation 7:14). Paul frequently used the words 'joy' and 'rejoicing' in connection with 'sufferings' or 'tribulation' (Romans 5:3; 12:12; 2 Corinthians 7:4).

Remember William Barclay's definition of *makarios* joy? 'Completely untouchable and unassailable . . . that joy that seeks us through our pain, that joy which sorrow and loss, and pain and grief, are powerless to touch, that joy which shines through tears, and which nothing in life or death can take away.'[5]

The bottom line on joy in Paul's great 'epistle of joy' is, 'I am ready for anything through the strength of the one who lives within me' (Philippians 4:13, J. B. Phillips); 'I can do everything with the help of Christ who gives me the strength I need' (NLT).

Paul's motto: 'I can – through Christ!' Not a bad motto for the contemporary Christian and for the contemporary Church.

If crisis lies ahead: for this we have Jesus.

The Christian has nothing to fear so long as he remembers the accessibility of the all-sufficient Saviour. The power of Christ within is sufficient for every crisis of life. Release this power by faith, and the fullness of joy Christ promised is yours.

'Most Christians . . . long for depth, for passion, for a satisfying peace and stability instead of a superficial relationship with God made up of words without feelings and struggles without healings. Surely there is more to the life of faith than church meetings, Bible study, religious jargon, and periodic prayers. Surely the awesome Spirit of God wishes to do more within us than what is presently going on!'[6] And there is a joy explosion He wants to cause in your life that will blast your complacency to kingdom come, put your congregation on a warfooting with the world – and prepare both the Church and the world to meet Christ the King.

[1]Martyn Lloyd-Jones, *Joy Unspeakable* (Kingsway, 1984), page 97. [2]Martyn Lloyd-Jones, *The Life of Joy* (Hodder, 1993), page 17. [3]Martyn Lloyd-Jones, *Joy unspeakable*, pages 97-113. [4]Ibid, pages 98-100. [5]William Barclay, *Daily Study Bible: The Gospel of Matthew*, volume 1 (St Andrew Press, 1956), page 84. [6]Charles R. Swindoll, *Flying Closer to the Flame* (Nelson Word, 1993), page 28.